first 15

Printed in Dallas, Texas by The Odee Company

Contact: contact@first15.org
www.first15.org

Layout Designed by Matt Ravenelle
mattravenelle.com

Images curated from
Unsplash

ABOUT FIRST15

Spending time alone with God every day can be a struggle. We're busier – and more stressed – than ever. But still, we know it's important to spend time alone with our Creator. We know we need to read his word, pray, and worship him.

First15 bridges the gap between desire and reality, helping you establish the rhythm of meaningful, daily experiences in God's presence. First15 answers the critical questions:

• Why should I spend time alone with God?
• How do I spend time alone with God?
• How do I get the most out of my time alone with God?
• How can I become more consistent with my time alone with God?

And by answering these questions through the format of daily devotionals, you'll practice the rhythm of meeting with God while experiencing the incredible gift of his loving presence given to those who make time to meet with him.

Allow God's passionate pursuit to draw you in across the next several days. And watch as every day is better than the last as your life is built on the solid foundation of God's love through the power of consistent, meaningful time alone with him.

To learn more about First15, visit our website first15. org. First15 is available across mobile app, email, podcast, and our website. Subscribe to our devotional today and experience God in a fresh way every day.

———————

ABOUT THE AUTHOR

Craig Denison is the author of First15, a daily devotional guiding over a million believers into a fresh experience with God every day. In 2015, Craig founded First15 after sensing a longing in God's heart for his people to be about relationship – real, restored relationship with him – that above all else, he simply wanted the hearts of his people. Craig began praying, dreaming, and writing. And the idea of helping people spend the first fifteen minutes of their day focusing on nothing else but growing in their relationship with God was born. The vision was birthed in Craig's heart that if we as a people would worship, read, and pray at the beginning of every day, everything could change for the better. Craig writes, speaks, and he and his wife, Rachel lead worship to help believers establish a more tangible, meaningful connection with God.

———

CONTENTS

The abundant life

"I came that they may have life and
have it abundantly." – John 10:10

WEEKLY OVERVIEW

Through the life, death, and resurrection of Jesus we have been afforded an opportunity to live an incredibly abundant life here on earth. Our God is nearer, more tangible, and has a greater ability to make his presence known than we've yet realized. He longs to make his children more in tune and aware of the depths of his love, guidance, empowerment, and nearness. He longs for our days here on earth to be marked by unveiled communion with him. As we look at what it is to live an abundant life here on earth, I pray that your heart will be awakened to the reality of God's presence and affection in your life.

God Cares About the Present

DEVOTIONAL

I used to view my relationship with God as a straight line of spiritual progress. My goal in spending time in the secret place with fellow believers at church and at work was to try and make the movement across this line of spiritual growth as quickly and painlessly as possible. I would get frustrated any time I got hung up on some issue or sin and couldn't experience freedom quickly enough. My time spent with Jesus was more about how he could change me than how deeply he already loves me.

We unfortunately live in a day and age where speed and progress is everything. We lose our patience as soon as a waiter takes too long to get us our check, a light takes an extra thirty seconds than we want it to, a driver holds us back five minutes from our destination, or a conversation interrupts the jam-packed schedule of our day. And painfully, we have allowed our culture to shape our perspective of God's heart for us rather than allowing his word and Spirit to reveal how incredibly patient he is.

1 Corinthians 13:4-7 says, *"Love is patient and kind; love does not envy or boast; it is not arrogant or rude. It does not insist on its own way; it is not irritable or resentful; it does not rejoice at wrongdoing, but rejoices with the truth. Love bears all things, believes all things, hopes all things, endures all things."* Every one of these aspects of love finds its perfect fulfillment in the heart of our Father. Our God is patient and kind. He bears our imperfections with love and grace, believes wholeheartedly in us, is filled with hope over who we are, and joyfully endures our process of sanctification.

"Therefore do not be anxious about tomorrow, for tomorrow will be anxious for itself. Sufficient for the day is its own trouble."

MATTHEW 6:34

13

You see, our heavenly Father cares deeply about you presently. He isn't waiting until you get a little holier to pour out the full depths of his love and joy over you. He isn't holding back the satisfaction he feels in simply living in relationship with you until you finally get over a certain sin. He loves and longs for unveiled communion with you right now.

If we wait until we have it all together to settle into the pace of this life, find peace, and fully enjoy God, we will never experience the wealth of abundant life available to us this side of heaven. Matthew 6:34 says, *"Therefore do not be anxious about tomorrow, for tomorrow will be anxious for itself. Sufficient for the day is its own trouble."* Have patience for yourself and others the way your heavenly Father does. Take time to receive his perfect perspective for today. Give your relationship with him all the energy you have and waste nothing on the frivolous cares of tomorrow.

Take time in guided prayer to allow your Father to overwhelm you with the love he feels for you right now, as you are. Experience today the peace and joy that can only be found when you surrender the entirety of your life, spiritual development, and future plans to your faithful Shepherd and simply follow him to green pastures and still waters. He promises there will be more green pastures tomorrow. He promises to guide you faithfully every day to the fullness of life he died to give you. Your only job as his sheep is to trust him, let him love and care for you, and follow his perfect leadership. May you drink deeply of the living waters of God's love today as you rest in the presence of your loving Shepherd.

14

GUIDED PRAYER

1. Meditate on God's patience and love for you in the present. Allow Scripture to guide you to a desire to encounter God fully and openly just as you are.

"Love is patient and kind; love does not envy or boast; it is not arrogant or rude. It does not insist on its own way; it is not irritable or resentful; it does not rejoice at wrongdoing, but rejoices with the truth. Love bears all things, believes all things, hopes all things, endures all things." 1 Corinthians 13:4-7

"Therefore do not be anxious, saying, 'What shall we eat?' or 'What shall we drink?' or 'What shall we wear?' For the Gentiles seek after all these things, and your heavenly Father knows that you need them all. But seek first the kingdom of God and his righteousness, and all these things will be added to you. Therefore do not be anxious about tomorrow, for tomorrow will be anxious for itself. Sufficient for the day is its own trouble." Matthew 6:31-34

2. What burden are you carrying that is grounded in the future instead of the present? What are you striving toward that is not found in the green pastures Jesus desires to lead you to today?

"You also, be patient. Establish your hearts, for the coming of the Lord is at hand." James 5:8

3. Ask the Holy Spirit to guide you into a lifestyle of living presently. Ask him what it looks like to cast off fear over tomorrow and experience the abundant life meant for you in the present. Take time to rest in the presence of God and discover his patience over you.

"Be still before the Lord and wait patiently for him." Psalm 37:7

"And let steadfastness have its full effect, that you may be perfect and complete, lacking in nothing." James 1:4

Your heavenly Father is most definitely molding and shaping you to look more like Jesus through a process of spiritual development. He has perfect plans for your sanctification that you might have a greater sense of his love at the end of every day. But that process is defined by daily living in the present and engaging with him fully in each moment. Leave the planning and leadership up to him, and simply follow him to green pastures and still waters every day. Seek relationship with him and allow daily, consistent encounters with him to mold and fashion you into a greater reflection of your Good Shepherd. May you find peace, joy, and patience by living in the present today.

Extended Reading: James 1

Choosing to Worship

DAY 2

DEVOTIONAL

In this life, we have an ability to choose to worship which we will never have again. When God brings final restoration to all things and we live in perfect communion with him, we will see him and know him fully. In heaven, worship will not be a choice. It will be the natural response of all of creation to the full revelation of God. Revelation 5:11-14 depicts this image:

Then I looked, and I heard around the throne and the living creatures and the elders the voice of many angels, numbering myriads of myriads and thousands of thousands, saying with a loud voice, "Worthy is the Lamb who was slain, to receive power and wealth and wisdom and might and honor and glory and blessing!" And I heard every creature in heaven and on earth and under the earth and in the sea, and all that is in them, saying, "To him who sits on the throne and to the Lamb be blessing and honor and glory and might forever and ever!" And the four living creatures said, "Amen!" and the elders fell down and worshiped.

God loves our worship here. John 4:23 says, *"But the hour is coming, and is now here, when the true worshipers will worship the Father in spirit and truth, for the Father is seeking such people to worship him."* Did you know that God is seeking your worship? It delights the heart of your Father when you desire to encounter him, know him, and give him your affections. There is nothing he loves more than communion with us.

"But the hour is coming, and is now here, when the true worshipers will worship the Father in spirit and truth, for the Father is seeking such people to worship him."

JOHN 4:23

When we choose to worship God here on earth, we are declaring to the Father and all of creation that he is King of kings and Lord of lords, and that he is our true ambition. To worship God here is to crown him as Lord of your life, come underneath his leadership, and make him first priority. What we do with our limited time here on earth has the power to affect the heart of God for all eternity. And living a lifestyle of worship instead of choosing the things of the world has the power to guide others into relationship with the Father, thereby changing the nature of their eternities forever.

Gathering together to worship with fellow believers is no small or fleeting task if we will take time to ask God what it does to his heart. Every time we gather together to worship, we can move the heart of our Father. We have the ability here on earth to delight our Creator. He sent Jesus to die that we might walk in communion with him. Our worship and pursuit of relationship with God is the reward for the unmerited suffering of our Savior. Every word we sing from our hearts matters. Every person we love is music to the ears of our Father. Every act of worship has eternal significance.

Take time in guided prayer to allow God to reveal his longing for your worship. Allow Scripture to fill you with a desire to worship with your life. Crown God as King and Lord and live to satisfy your God's desire for continual, intimate relationship with you.

GUIDED PRAYER

1. Meditate on the value of your worship here on earth. Allow Scripture and God's presence to stir you up to live a lifestyle of devoted worship right now.

"You have said, 'Seek my face.' My heart says to you, 'Your face, Lord, do I seek.'" Psalm 27:8

"Ascribe to the Lord the glory due his name; worship the Lord in the splendor of holiness." Psalm 29:2

"Then I looked, and I heard around the throne and the living creatures and the elders the voice of many angels, numbering myriads of myriads and thousands of thousands, saying with a loud voice, 'Worthy is the Lamb who was slain, to receive power and wealth and wisdom and might and honor and glory and blessing!' And I heard every creature in heaven and on earth and under the earth and in the sea, and all that is in them, saying, 'To him who sits on the throne and to the Lamb be blessing and honor and glory and might forever and ever!' And the four living creatures said, 'Amen!' and the elders fell down and worshiped." Revelation 5:11–14

2. What have you been pursuing above worshipping God? What is keeping you from doing everything in your life as an act of worship?

3. Ask God to show you how much he loves your worship. Ask him to help you live a lifestyle of worship, daily surrendering all you do to him as an act of praise and love. Rest in his presence and spend time simply being with him.

Mark 14 describes for us an inspiring story of worship. Mark 14:3-6 says, *"And while he was at Bethany in the house of Simon the leper, as he was reclining at table, a woman came with an alabaster flask of ointment of pure nard, very costly, and she broke the flask and poured it over his head. There were some who said to themselves indignantly, 'Why was the ointment wasted like that? For this ointment could have been sold for more than three hundred denarii and given to the poor.' And they scolded her. But Jesus said, 'Leave her alone. Why do you trouble her? She has done a beautiful thing to me.'"* And then later in verse 9 Jesus says, *"And truly, I say to you, wherever the gospel is proclaimed in the whole world, what she has done will be told in memory of her."* This woman's worship affected eternity. Her story of devotion and affection for Jesus has inspired countless Christians. May we live like this woman. May we give all that we have in love and devotion to the King who gave everything for us.

Extended Reading: Psalm 27

Glorious Relationship

DEVOTIONAL

There is a wealth of glorious relationship available to us on earth that we have yet to fully experience. Jesus has made a way for us to have restored relationship with our heavenly Father again, not only in heaven, but right now. We have been washed clean by the blood of the pure and spotless Lamb so that the presence

"Behold, I stand at the door and knock. If anyone hears my voice and opens the door, I will come in to him and eat with him, and he with me."

REVELATION 3:20

of the living God now resides with us. God is here, and he is ready for you and me to experience the fullness of life only found in continual communion with him.

Revelation 3:20 says, *"Behold, I stand at the door and knock. If anyone hears my voice and opens the door, I will come in to him and eat with him, and he with me."* God is continually knocking on the doors of our hearts, ready and willing to come in and meet with us in every part of our lives. Each of us are created for intimacy, free from shame and rejection. We live unsatisfied until our hearts find their home with our loving and present Father.

God is knocking on the door of your heart today and asking you to allow him to come in and fill you with the life of glorious relationship. He longs to breathe into your frame of dust so that the dry and weary places of your heart are filled to overflowing with the living waters of his love. Psalm 139:1-6 says,

O Lord, you have searched me and known me! You know when I sit down and when I rise up; you discern my thoughts from afar. You search out my path and my lying down and are acquainted with all my ways. Even before a word is

on my tongue, behold, O Lord, you know it altogether. You hem me in, behind and before, and lay your hand upon me. Such knowledge is too wonderful for me; it is high; I cannot attain it.

God is always available, always ready, and always willing to guide you into an encounter with him. All that is required of you is an open heart. True life here on earth finds its roots solely in restored relationship with the Creator. There is no good apart from the Lord (Psalm 16:2). There is no love like the one we have found in God. There is no friend like the Holy Spirit. There is no purpose like wholeheartedly pursuing the fullness of relationship available with God.

Zephaniah 3:17 says, *"The Lord your God is in your midst, a mighty one who will save; he will rejoice over you with gladness; he will quiet you by his love; he will exult over you with loud singing."* Take time to allow God to rejoice over you. Allow him to quiet the stress and cares of this life with his loving presence. Ask him to reveal to you just how near he is. And live today in light of the glorious relationship with your heavenly Father made available to you by the powerful sacrifice of Jesus.

GUIDED PRAYER

1. Meditate on the wealth of relationship available to you with God. Allow Scripture to fill you with a desire to have more consistent encounters with your heavenly Father.

"How precious to me are your thoughts, O God! How vast is the sum of them! If I would count them, they are more than the sand. I awake, and I am still with you." Psalm 139:17-18

"Can a woman forget her nursing child, that she should have no compassion on the son of her womb? Even these may forget, yet I will not forget you." Isaiah 49:15

"Behold, I stand at the door and knock. If anyone hears my voice and opens the door, I will come in to him and eat with him, and he with me." Revelation 3:20

2. In what ways are you not experiencing the fullness of life available to you in God? Where do you need more encounters with God's presence and love?

3. Take time to simply let God love you. Open the door of your heart to your heavenly Father, and let him come meet with you. Have faith that he will guide you into an encounter with himself today and give you exactly what you need. May you find refreshment and revitalization in the loving embrace of your Father.

"Draw near to God, and he will draw near to you." James 4:8

"And without faith it is impossible to please him, for whoever would draw near to God must believe that he exists and that he rewards those who seek him." Hebrews 11:6

May the words of Jesus in John 15:4-6 fill you with a desire to stay in communion with your heavenly Father throughout everything you do today:

Abide in me, and I in you. As the branch cannot bear fruit by itself, unless it abides in the vine, neither can you, unless you abide in me. I am the vine; you are the branches. Whoever abides in me and I in him, he it is that bears much fruit, for apart from me you can do nothing. If anyone does not abide in me he is thrown away like a branch and withers; and the branches are gathered, thrown into the fire, and burned.

Extended Reading: Psalm 139

Passionate Pursuit

DAY 4

DEVOTIONAL

The key to abundant life here on earth is the passionate pursuit of Jesus. I doubt there will be a single believer who ever reads these words that will doubt that statement. But I also know that we often fail to truly believe that statement in our hearts. If we truly believed

"You have said, 'Seek my face.' My heart says to you, 'Your face, Lord, do I seek.'"

that the key to abundant life was passionately pursuing Jesus, most of our lives would look drastically different. My life would look drastically different.

If we truly believed that passionately pursuing Jesus would bring us abundant life, the way we spend our time would drastically change. We would choose pursuing the presence of God over entertainment more often. We would structure most of our worship services differently. We would cease working for the opinion of man and start living for the good pleasure of our Creator. And our lives would look simpler, more joyful, more peaceful, and more like the life of Jesus.

The good news for you and me is that there is grace for us today. Isaiah 55:6-7 says, *"Seek the Lord while he may be found; call upon him while he is near; let the wicked forsake his way, and the unrighteous man his thoughts; let him return to the Lord, that he may have compassion on him, and to our God, for he will abundantly pardon."* It's time for the people of God to wake up to the true purpose for our lives. It's time that we stop seeking the things of the world and give our lives to the total and wholehearted pursuit of Jesus. And there is grace from on high that God longs to give us today to do so.

The Lord is saying to you and me, *"Seek my face"* (Psalm 27:8). And we need to reply as David by saying, *"My heart says to you, 'Your face, Lord, do I seek'"* (Psalm 27:8). All that stands between you and a radical life transformation is turning away from the cares and pursuits of the world and giving your heart to your heavenly Father. We have a daily opportunity to live in total communion with our Creator, receiving and giving love in everything we do. Jesus paid the ultimate price for you and me to live with the tangible knowledge of God's love for us. We also have the opportunity every day to live marginal lives where we experience and commune with God part of the time and live for the fleeting and unsatisfying ways of the world the other. The choice is yours today. Will you passionately pursue relationship with Jesus, or will you allow the ways of this world to crowd out parts of your life like weeds blocking you from the refreshing, life-giving presence of the living God?

Take time in guided prayer to listen to your Father, meditate on his promise of abundant life, and chase after wholehearted relationship with Jesus at all costs. May you experience to new levels today the abundant life Jesus died to give you.

25

GUIDED PRAYER

1. Meditate on the importance of passionately pursuing relationship with Jesus above all else. Allow Scripture to fill you with the will to choose God over the things of the world today.

"The young lions suffer want and hunger; but those who seek the Lord lack no good thing." Psalm 34:10

"Then you will call upon me and come and pray to me, and I will hear you. You will seek me and find me, when you seek me with all your heart. I will be found by you, declares the Lord, and I will restore your fortunes and gather you from all the nations and all the places where I have driven you, declares the Lord, and I will bring you back to the place from which I sent you into exile." Jeremiah 29:12-14

"But seek first the kingdom of God and his righteousness, and all these things will be added to you." Matthew 6:33

2. What have you been pursuing above relationship with Jesus? What has been holding you back from seeking wholehearted relationship with God above all else?

3. Ask the Lord to help you live for him alone today. Take time to receive his presence and receive his incredible, grace-filled love for you. Enjoy his presence and allow it to lay a foundation on which you seek the Lord wholeheartedly.

"You have said, 'Seek my face.' My heart says to you, 'Your face, Lord, do I seek.'" Psalm 27:8

"Seek the Lord and his strength; seek his presence continually!" 1 Chronicles 16:11

"O God, you are my God; earnestly I seek you; my soul thirsts for you; my flesh faints for you, as in a dry and weary land where there is no water." Psalm 63:1

True passion for God is always kindled as a response to the catalytic love of God. His passion for us, his pursuit of us, ignites a flame in our hearts that the world can't put out. If you begin to feel passionless, lukewarm in your faith, ask God for a fresh experience with his love. Ask him to remind you of his goodness, his provision, his pursuit. And allow his love to reignite the flame of your heart, that you would live with wholehearted devotion to him. May you discover new passion for God in your life today as your eyes are opened to all the incredible ways he's at work in you and around you.

Extended Reading: Psalm 84

Eternal Impact

DEVOTIONAL

You and I were created to make an eternal impact that no one else can make. We've each been given a destiny of good works that are incredibly important and wholly unique. No one else can touch people's lives like you can. God created you for a unique purpose that is solely yours, and he is ready today to equip and empower you to make a deep and lasting impact on this earth.

*"For we are his workmanship, created in
Christ Jesus for good works, which God prepared
beforehand, that we should walk in them."*

EPHESIANS 2:10

Ephesians 2:10 says, *"For we are his workmanship, created in Christ Jesus for good works, which God prepared beforehand, that we should walk in them."* You are the workmanship of the Master Craftsman. You are the creation of the Almighty Creator of all. And he has made you for such a time as this. You are not here by mistake. You are not less than other believers around you. Your calling and anointing carries no less weight or importance in the kingdom than anyone else's.

As a Christian, you have been made new. The person you were before believing in Jesus has been redeemed and transformed. You now have the same Holy Spirit dwelling within you who raised Jesus from the grave, empowered the disciples to save, heal, and set free the lost, and authored the words of Scripture.

Making an eternal impact is all about you becoming and living out of who you are in Christ Jesus. It's about adopting the new creation that you have become through the power of Jesus' life, death, and resurrection. 1 Peter 2:9-10 says,

But you are a chosen race, a royal priesthood, a holy nation, a people for his own possession, that you may proclaim the excellencies of him who called you out of darkness into his marvelous light. Once you were not a people, but now you are God's people; once you had not received mercy, but now you have received mercy.

Making an eternal impact is less about you and more about the *"excellencies of him who called you out of darkness into his marvelous light."* It's about proclaiming with your life the depth of power, love, grace, transformation, and forgiveness your heavenly Father has toward all who believe. You belong to the King of kings and Lord of lords. He is with you always and is ready to empower you for a life of eternal impact. There is no greater life than one seeing the world transformed by the love of its Creator.

Take time in guided prayer to ask God to fill you and empower you with his love, to reveal to you the impact he longs for you to make today, and to help you choose to live out of the new creation you are in Jesus.

29

GUIDED PRAYER

1. Meditate on the importance of making an eternal impact.

Reflect on the goodness of working with the Holy Spirit to transform the earth around you with God's redeeming love.

"In the same way, let your light shine before others, so that they may see your good works and give glory to your Father who is in heaven." Matthew 5:16

"But you are a chosen race, a royal priesthood, a holy nation, a people for his own possession, that you may proclaim the excellencies of him who called you out of darkness into his marvelous light. Once you were not a people, but now you are God's people; once you had not received mercy, but now you have received mercy." 1 Peter 2:9-10

"Who gave himself for us to redeem us from all lawlessness and to purify for himself a people for his own possession who are zealous for good works." Titus 2:14

2. Ask the Holy Spirit to reveal to you the plans he has for you

today. What good works have been prepared for you beforehand? How can you change the world with the message of God's grace and love?

"For we are his workmanship, created in Christ Jesus for good works, which God prepared beforehand, that we should walk in them." Ephesians 2:10

3. Ask God to help you live out of the new creation you are in Jesus.

Ask him to lead you away from temptation and toward the fullness of his presence that you might see his kingdom come to earth in all you do.

Making an eternal impact is really all about love. The world is looking for love. Love sets us free from the bonds of worldliness. Love empowers us to live for heaven over the pursuits of the world. And it's love that will draw the lost into the fold of God. Allow the Lord to fill you with love for others around you. Ask him to give you his heart for those in desperate need of a revelation of his love. Follow the Spirit and live today to make an eternal impact with the message of God's grace and love for all he has made (Psalm 145:9).

Extended Reading: 1 Corinthians 13

Healed, Transformed, Freed

DEVOTIONAL

Too often we as believers settle for lives less than what God intends for us. God has the desire and ability to do far greater than we could ever ask or imagine (Ephesians 3:20). He longs for us to live healed, transformed, and set free from the bonds of sin and slavery to the world. As we look at God's plans for healing, transformation, and freedom today, I pray that you will be filled with a hunger for the fullness of life available to you in Christ Jesus.

Jesus spent most of his ministry doing powerful works of physical and emotional healing. And once he ascended to heaven he passed on the ministry of healing to his disciples and empowered them to do even greater works (John 14:12). God has never stopped his pursuit of healing the ailments and hearts of those he loves.

"Bless the Lord, O my soul, and forget not all his benefits, who forgives all your iniquity, who heals all your diseases, who redeems your life from the pit, who crowns you with steadfast love and mercy."

PSALM 103:2-4

Too often we allow the wounds of this world to settle in our hearts and dictate the way we live our lives. We agree with the lie that the pains of our past are just part of life and that true courage is taking what has hurt us, pulling ourselves up with our own strength, and pressing forward. The heart of our God is for the healing of those wounds. Psalm 147:3 plainly says, *"He heals the brokenhearted and binds up their wounds."* God longs to meet you at the place of your wounds and provide healing today. He longs to reveal to you his heart for your pain, fill you with his loving presence, and walk with you through the process of healing. Choose healing for your wounds today that you might live with more abundant joy and peace instead of heartache and pain.

Our God is a God of transformation. He loves us where we are but cares for us too deeply to let us live with the lies, perspectives, and pursuits that rob us from the abundant life Jesus died to give us. Romans 12:2 says, *"Do not be conformed to this world, but be transformed by the renewal of your mind, that by testing you may discern what is the will of God, what is good and acceptable and perfect."* God longs to renew your mind to the truth of his love, nearness, power, and grace. He longs to transform you into a better reflection of Jesus that you might live to the fullest. He longs to fill you with longings and passions that will guide you to a life of purpose and eternal impact. Say yes to being transformed by God's Spirit and word that you might experience the abundant life only available in God.

Lastly, God longs for you to live this life freed from the sins and ways of this world. 1 Peter 2:16 says, *"Live as people who are free, not using your freedom as a cover-up for evil, but living as servants of God."* Galatians 5:1 says, *"For freedom Christ has set us free; stand firm therefore, and do not submit again to a yoke of slavery."* 2 Corinthians 3:17 says, *"Now the Lord is the Spirit, and where the Spirit of the Lord is, there is freedom."* Freedom has been bought for you by the blood of the Lamb. You are no longer a slave to this world but a slave to righteousness. In the Holy Spirit you have freedom from every past pursuit and present temptation if you will simply follow his guidance into a lifestyle of righteousness. Choose freedom today. Choose to follow the Spirit away from that which will lead you to sin and toward that which will fill you with a longing for holiness.

Take time in guided prayer to meditate on Scripture and pursue wholeheartedly a lifestyle of healing, transformation, and freedom with the help of your heavenly Father.

33

GUIDED PRAYER

1. Meditate on the importance and availability of living healed, transformed, and freed.

"He himself bore our sins in his body on the tree, that we might die to sin and live to righteousness. By his wounds you have been healed." 1 Peter 2:24

"And we all, with unveiled face, beholding the glory of the Lord, are being transformed into the same image from one degree of glory to another. For this comes from the Lord who is the Spirit." 2 Corinthians 3:18

"Live as people who are free, not using your freedom as a cover-up for evil, but living as servants of God." 1 Peter 2:16

2. Where do you need healing, transformation, and freedom today?

3. Ask the Lord for whatever it is you need. Trust in his goodness and have faith that he will provide for you everything you need when you ask it of him.

"Bless the Lord, O my soul, and forget not all his benefits, who forgives all your iniquity, who heals all your diseases, who redeems your life from the pit, who crowns you with steadfast love and mercy." Psalm 103:2-4

"Therefore I tell you, whatever you ask in prayer, believe that you have received it, and it will be yours." Mark 11:24

"And this is the confidence that we have toward him, that if we ask anything according to his will he hears us. And if we know that he hears us in whatever we ask, we know that we have the requests that we have asked of him." 1 John 5:14-15

May we not be children who settle for anything less than all our heavenly Father has for us. May we listen to and receive all the wealth of truth, love, and grace our God longs to lavish upon us. Pursue with your whole heart the life God intends for you. And live today out of the revelation that your God is leading you to stiller waters and greener pastures than you have yet known.

Extended Reading: Psalm 103

Eternity
Right Now

DAY 7

DEVOTIONAL

You and I are living in eternity—right now. Eternal life doesn't start when we take our last breath here. You and I are currently experiencing eternal life in relationship with our Father. C.S. Lewis said in *The Weight of Glory*, "There are no ordinary people. You have never talked to a mere mortal. Nations, cultures, arts, civilizations—these are mortal, and their life is to ours as the life of a gnat." Ecclesiastes 3:11 says it this way, *"He has made everything beautiful in its time. Also, he has put eternity into man's heart, yet so that he cannot find out what God has done from the beginning to the end."*

"He has made everything beautiful in its time. Also, he has put eternity into man's heart, yet so that he cannot find out what God has done from the beginning to the end."

ECCLESIASTES 3:11

What does it mean for you and me to live in eternity right now? What would it look like for us to have a perspective that looks past the fleeting and temporal nature of this world to the never-ending line of eternity to which we truly belong?

Having an eternal perspective causes me to live drastically differently. My heart burns to live out of obedience to passages like Matthew 6:19-21 where Jesus teaches, *"Do not lay up for yourselves treasures on earth, where moth and rust destroy and where thieves break in and steal, but lay up for yourselves treasures in heaven, where neither moth nor rust destroys and where thieves do not break in and steal. For where your treasure is, there your heart will be also."* The way we live right now impacts our eternity. The way we pursue the things of God impacts what our experience will be like when heaven and earth pass away and God ushers in the new age of true face-to-face communion with him.

The time has come for us to set aside that which entangles us to the fate of this age and live for that which is eternal. The time has come for us to stop seeking fulfillment from that which is fleeting and instead pursue true abundant life here on earth by giving our heart fully to the Father. Galatians 6:8 says,

"For the one who sows to his own flesh will from the flesh reap corruption, but the one who sows to the Spirit will from the Spirit reap eternal life." Where are you sowing your time, energy, resources, and heart? What treasure have you stored up with your loving, good heavenly Father? What are you doing to impact eternity?

Psalm 102:25-27 says, *"Of old you laid the foundation of the earth, and the heavens are the work of your hands. They will perish, but you will remain; they will all wear out like a garment. You will change them like a robe, and they will pass away, but you are the same, and your years have no end."* We worship a God who sees all of eternity at a glance. He dwells within the whole scope of eternity seamlessly and fully. He is the God of your past, present, and future. To give your life to him and his will is to invest in that which will fully satisfy the desires of your heart for all time. The God who has formed you knows that which will make your heart truly happy, and he is calling you to step away from the fulfillment of this age and to pursue wholeheartedly the purposes and plans of his kingdom. May you invest your affections, time, resources, and heart with your loving and kind Father. May you live for eternity and rid yourself of the burden and weight of this world. And may you experience today the abundant life that comes from acknowledging the eternal nature of all you do.

37

GUIDED PRAYER

1. Meditate on the eternal destiny to which you belong. Think about what heaven will be like. Allow Scripture to stir up your desire to live for heaven rather than the things of the world.

"Truly, truly, I say to you, whoever hears my word and believes him who sent me has eternal life. He does not come into judgment, but has passed from death to life." John 5:24

"In my Father's house are many rooms. If it were not so, would I have told you that I go to prepare a place for you?" John 14:2

"But as it is, they desire a better country, that is, a heavenly one. Therefore God is not ashamed to be called their God, for he has prepared for them a city." Hebrews 11:16

2. Where in your life could you adopt a more eternal perspective? Where are you living for the fleeting and temporal instead of the eternal?

"Do not lay up for yourselves treasures on earth, where moth and rust destroy and where thieves break in and steal, but lay up for yourselves treasures in heaven, where neither moth nor rust destroys and where thieves

do not break in and steal. For where your treasure is, there your heart will be also." Matthew 6:19-21

3. Take time to rest in the presence of the God who dwells in eternity. Allow him to fill you, refresh you, and revive you. Ask him to fill you with a desire to pursue eternity with greater fervor.

"Repent therefore, and turn back, that your sins may be blotted out, that times of refreshing may come from the presence of the Lord, and that he may send the Christ appointed for you, Jesus, whom heaven must receive until the time for restoring all the things about which God spoke by the mouth of his holy prophets long ago." Acts 3:19-21

May Isaiah 57:15 fill you with praise and wonder for the God you serve and love:

"For thus says the One who is high and lifted up, who inhabits eternity, whose name is Holy: "I dwell in the high and holy place, and also with him who is of a contrite and lowly spirit, to revive the spirit of the lowly, and to revive the heart of the contrite."

Extended Reading: Hebrews 11

Seeking God

"You have said, 'Seek my face.' My heart says to you, 'Your face, Lord, do I seek.'" –Psalm 27:8

WEEKLY OVERVIEW

Learning to seek the face of God is the foundation for experiencing the amazing life Jesus died to give us. We have available to us through Christ all the wonders, excellencies, and satisfaction we can fathom. God has granted us grace upon grace, mercy upon mercy, affection upon affection, and love upon love. When we pursue him through all the avenues available to us, a door is opened in which we discover all our heavenly Father longs to give us. May you grow in your pursuit of God this week as we study various ways we've been given to seek his face.

Seeking God through Worship

DEVOTIONAL

Worship through song is one of the most powerful ways to connect directly to the love, compassion, power, and grace of God. In worship, walls we've placed between God and us get torn down, just as God tore the veil at the death of Christ. In worship, our hearts become soft, aware, and open to the glorious majesties of God's nearness. In worship, God makes his nearness known to us and fills us anew with the power of his manifest presence.

The Psalms are filled with exhortations to worship. Psalm 95:1-3 says, *"Oh come, let us sing to the Lord; let us make a joyful noise to the rock of our salvation! Let us come into his presence with thanksgiving; let us make a joyful noise to him with songs of praise! For the Lord is a great God, and a great King above all gods."* We are created to worship our Creator. When we give glory to God, we place him on the throne of our hearts and posture ourselves in the only position in which we will find peace: one of submission and humility. In the act of worship, we lay down everything we've allowed to matter more than God's perfect will for us and receive the grace to love him above all else.

Psalm 132:7 says, *"Let us go to his dwelling place; let us worship at his footstool!"* When we worship, we enter into direct contact with our all-powerful, all-loving, all-knowing heavenly Father. God's desire in worship

"Let us go to his dwelling
place; let us worship at his footstool!"

PSALM 132:7

is to draw us near to himself, fill us to overflow with his love, and wait patiently for us to love him in return. The more often we receive his love through worship, the more consistently we will love and honor him in all we do. I fear that many Christians engage in worship because they feel they should or are allotted a time in church to do so, but all the while never really desire to worship God. God is not a prideful King who demands inauthentic praise from his people. He is in no way insecure or needy. He is simply after true communion with you where he loves you and you love him in return. And he will keep loving you, speaking to you, and reminding you of his desire for you until you open your heart and realize that loving him is the most satisfying, fulfilling, and purposeful way to live.

My favorite way to engage in worship, either in my personal devotional time or in a corporate gathering, is to begin by opening my heart and asking the Holy Spirit to help me receive God's affection for me. 1 John 4:19 says, *"We love because he first loved us."* I forget too easily how deeply God loves me. As I go throughout my week, the cares of the world seem to creep in and rob me of a full understanding of the depths of God's love. So, I continually need reminders of his love that I may live my life in response to him rather than singing just because I should. Before you engage in worship, take a minute or two to reflect on God's love. Read a Psalm or a part of the gospel that will remind you of how much God loves you.

Ask God to speak to you and pour his love out on you. It isn't selfish to ask God to love you. He knows that we are in desperate need of his love, and he fully understands that we cannot love him without receiving his love first.

Richard J. Foster says it this way in his book, *Celebration of Discipline*:

"Worship is our response to the overtures of love from the heart of the Father. Its central reality is found "in Spirit and in Truth." It is kindled within us only when then the Spirit of God touches our human Spirit. Forms and rituals do not produce worship, nor does the formal disuse of forms and rituals. We can use all the right techniques and methods, we can have the best possible liturgy but we have not worshiped the Lord until Spirit touches Spirit. Singing, praying, praising, all may lead to worship, but worship is more than any of them. Our Spirit must be ignited by divine fire."

Whether or not you have encountered the miracle of God's presence in worship up to this day, God wants to draw you into a fresh and needed experience of his nearness right now. He wants to pour out his love on every dry and weary place of your heart. Take time in prayer to receive his love, allow his Spirit to touch your spirit, and respond to him with adoration.

47

GUIDED PRAYER

1. Meditate on the depths of God's love for you.

"But God shows his love for us in that while we were still sinners, Christ died for us." Romans 5:8

"No, in all these things we are more than conquerors through him who loved us. For I am sure that neither death nor life, nor angels nor rulers, nor things present nor things to come, nor powers, nor height nor depth, nor anything else in all creation, will be able to separate us from the love of God in Christ Jesus our Lord." Romans 8:37–39

"Your steadfast love, O Lord, extends to the heavens, your faithfulness to the clouds." Psalm 36:5

2. Ask the Holy Spirit to lead you into a direct encounter with God. Open your heart to the Holy Spirit and allow him to fill you with a knowledge of God's love and nearness. Wait on him and allow his Spirit to touch your spirit.

3. Respond to God's love with your own. Thank him for what he has done for you. Go through all the good things in your life, and give him adoration for them! Love him in whatever way you desire. If you're unsure of what to do, ask the Holy Spirit to fill you with a specific way to love God.

Richard Foster also wrote, "As worship begins in holy expectancy, it ends in holy obedience. Holy obedience saves worship from becoming an opiate, an escape from the pressing needs of modern life." Live today following the guidance of God's Spirit and his word. Respond to his love with your own loving obedience. May you discover the wealth of abundant life available to you through receiving God's love and loving him in return through the gift of worship.

Extended Reading: Psalm 132

Seeking God through Scripture

DAY 9

DEVOTIONAL

The pages of Scripture are filled with declarations of the wonderful, mysterious, powerful, and loving nature of our heavenly Father. Scripture is one of God's greatest gifts to his people, who so easily forget the labor of love he has undergone to gain restored relationship with us. The Bible is a companion to those who long to seek and find the invisible God who so

"Man shall not live by bread alone, but by every word that comes from the mouth of God."

MATTHEW 4:4

greatly desires to be discovered. Let's open our hearts today to Scripture and the Holy Spirit and receive fresh revelation on how God longs to use his word to guide us as we seek his face.

In Matthew 4:4 Jesus says, *"Man shall not live by bread alone, but by every word that comes from the mouth of God."* Scripture is meant to fill us with life by leading us directly to our heavenly Father. The power of Scripture lies in the fact that its pages are filled with the words of a God who is still active, powerful, and loving. I went years using Scripture incorrectly. I viewed it as a set of rules I needed to read and try to keep rather than as a guide to experiencing the adventure of communion with my heavenly Father. I viewed Scripture as a chore rather than the words of God meant specifically for me. I finally came to the realization that if I wanted to read the Bible, I would be. My problem wasn't a lack of will but rather a lack of revelation on God's intention behind authoring the Bible. My problem was that I hadn't experienced a life lived *"by every word that comes from the mouth of God."*

Wherever you are in your understanding of Scripture, know that God has fresh desire for his word in store for you today. He longs to fill you with a desire to read the words that will guide you to abundant life. The Holy Spirit longs to speak directly to you through words written thousands of years ago. Our Bible is a powerful miracle safeguarded for the benefit of all who would use it to seek the face of its Creator. May we all have the heart of the Psalmist and grow in our love of Scripture and the God who inspired it:

Oh how I love your law! It is my meditation all the day. Your commandment makes me wiser than my enemies, for it is ever with me. I have more understanding than all my teachers, for your testimonies are my meditation. I understand more than the aged, for I keep your precepts. I hold back my feet from every evil way, in order to keep your word. I do not turn aside from your rules, for you have taught me. How sweet are your words to my taste, sweeter than honey to my mouth! Through your precepts I get understanding; therefore I hate every false way (Psalm 119: 97-104).

GUIDED PRAYER

1. Meditate on the power of Scripture in seeking God.

"If you keep my commandments, you will abide in my love, just as I have kept my Father's commandments and abide in his love. These things I have spoken to you, that my joy may be in you, and that your joy may be full." John 15:10-11

"Man shall not live by bread alone, but by every word that comes from the mouth of God." Matthew 4:4

2. Where do you need the help of Scripture in seeking God? What lie do you believe about the character of God? What thought or perspective is keeping you from pursuing God with all your heart? Scripture is a powerful tool to combat incorrect thinking with God's truth.

3. Ask the Spirit to guide you to a passage of Scripture that will speak directly to your situation. Pay attention for a passage or book that comes to mind, or search online for key verses.

May you have ears to hear the voice of God speaking to you through the pages of Scripture. May your heart become soft and open to God's presence as you open his word. And may you experience the delight that comes from the knowledge of God's will for you as found in the pages of the Bible.

Extended Reading: Psalm 19

Seeking God through Prayer

DAY 10

DEVOTIONAL

The fact that God listens to us as his children changes the landscape of prayer from empty phrases uttered into the abyss to direct communication with the Creator and Sustainer of all. When you pray you are heard by your heavenly Father. And it's because he listens to us that prayer is one of the most wonderful and powerful avenues to pursue him. May we learn to dialogue in greater ways with our heavenly Father as we open our hearts to all he would show us today about prayer.

*"But when you pray, go into your
room and shut the door and pray to your
Father who is in secret."*

MATTHEW 6:6

Matthew 6:7-8 says, *"And when you pray, do not heap up empty phrases as the Gentiles do, for they think that they will be heard for their many words. Do not be like them, for your Father knows what you need before you ask him."* Jesus inaugurated an entirely new perspective on prayer. Prior to Jesus, God's people would pray out of obligation or ritual, begging a seemingly distant God to move on their behalf. Jesus taught that God knows our needs before we even ask. He taught that God is a good Father who longs to respond to the needs of his children. And in John 15:7 he taught, *"If you abide in me, and my words abide in you, ask whatever you wish, and it will be done for you."* God's desire is to respond favorably to our prayers. He always has our absolute best in mind and longs to satisfy the desires of our hearts.

The key to effective communication with God is first to trust that he is a good Father who listens and longs to answer the prayers of his children. After gaining proper perspective, we need to spend significant time allowing God to fill us with his desires for us, fashioning our hearts into a reflection of his. God will not give you what he knows is less than his best. Rather, he longs to fill you with a desire for what is best for you, then come along and satisfy that desire in magnificent and miraculous ways as you pray.

Jeremiah 33:3 says, *"Call to me and I will answer you, and will tell you great and hidden things that you have not known."* When you call out to your heavenly Father, trust that he will answer you. He longs to fill you with the knowledge and desire for his will. He longs to speak with you. You can have his heart and know how he feels. The Holy Spirit who dwells within you longs to reveal to you the perfect plans of your heavenly Father.

Spend time in prayer listening for the heartbeat of God and allowing him to fill you with the knowledge of his will.

GUIDED PRAYER

1. Meditate on God's purposes for prayer. Allow Scripture to fill you with trust and faith in God's ability to both listen and speak to you.

"And when you pray, do not heap up empty phrases as the Gentiles do, for they think that they will be heard for their many words. Do not be like them, for your Father knows what you need before you ask him." Matthew 6:7-8

"If you abide in me, and my words abide in you, ask whatever you wish, and it will be done for you." John 15:7

"My sheep hear my voice, and I know them, and they follow me." John 10:27

2. Ask the Spirit to fill you with a knowledge of God's desires for you. Where do you need God's wisdom? What part of your life doesn't seem to be marked by the work of God? Where do you need peace, joy, and purpose?

"Call to me and I will answer you, and will tell you great and hidden things that you have not known." Jeremiah 33:3

"Let me hear what God the Lord will speak, for he will speak peace to his people, to his saints; but let them not turn back to folly." Psalm 85:8

3. Pray in accordance with God's will. Pray with boldness after you discover God's heart for your need, knowing that he hears you and will respond to your prayer perfectly.

In his book, *Power through Prayer*, E. M. Bounds shares incredible wisdom on a lifestyle of prayer. May his words guide you into a deeper connection with your heavenly Father today:

"The men who have done the most for God in this world have been early on their knees. He who fritters away the early morning, its opportunity and freshness, in other pursuits than seeking God will make poor headway seeking Him the rest of the day. If God is not first in our thoughts and efforts in the morning, He will be in the last place the remainder of the day."

Extended Reading: Matthew 6

Seeking God through Fasting

DAY 11

DEVOTIONAL

In his book, *A Hunger for God*, John Piper writes, "If you don't feel strong desires for the manifestation of the glory of God, it is not because you have drunk deeply and are satisfied. It is because you have nibbled so long at the table of the world. Your soul is stuffed with small things, and there is no room for the great." Fasting is a powerful tool for placing anything that entangles us to the depravity and longings of this world in proper perspective. It builds for us a seat at the table of

*"So we fasted and implored our God for
this, and he listened to our entreaty."*

EZRA 8:23

God where we can drink deeply of the wonders and satisfaction found in restored relationship with our heavenly Father. May the Lord reveal to you the places in your heart which need to be realigned as we look at all God longs to do in us through the gift of fasting.

Matthew 6:16-18 says, *"And when you fast, do not look gloomy like the hypocrites, for they disfigure their faces that their fasting may be seen by others. Truly, I say to you, they have received their reward. But when you fast, anoint your head and wash your face, that your fasting may not be seen by others but by your Father who is in secret. And your Father who sees in secret will reward you."* Fasting is a secret declaration to yourself and your heavenly Father that you want more of what he has to give you. It's a private plea for the abundant life that can only be found in more of God and less of the world. And God responds to our pleas with his glory and grace causing the cares of this world to pale in comparison to the abundance of God's love.

There's something powerful that takes place when we willingly surrender satisfaction in the world to make space for more of God. God loves to respond to our hunger. In his patience he waits for us to cry out to him to bring us into the fullness of what he has for us. But in his pursuit of us he constantly whispers from his Spirit to ours, beckoning us to give up the rags of this world for the riches that come through the life, death, and resurrection of Jesus.

Whether you're fasting food, entertainment, relationships, or anything else to make space for more of God, the intention of God for fasting is to fill you up to overflow. It's his intention to realign your life to position you to consistently receive all he has for you. It's his intention to transform the pangs of separation from whatever you're fasting into deep prayers for more of his goodness. May you be honest with yourself and be filled with the desire to fast from that which stands in the way of you fully living the abundant life.

GUIDED PRAYER

1. Meditate on God's desire for fasting. Allow truth to form your perspective on this age-old discipline.

"So we fasted and implored our God for this, and he listened to our entreaty." Ezra 8:23

"If you don't feel strong desires for the manifestation of the glory of God, it is not because you have drunk deeply and are satisfied. It is because you have nibbled so long at the table of the world. Your soul is stuffed with small things, and there is no room for the great." — John Piper, *A Hunger For God*

2. What do you need to fast? What's holding you back from the fullness God longs to give you? What could you give up to create more space for relationship with him? Be honest with yourself and God. Ask the Holy Spirit to reveal places in your life that need the transformation that comes through fasting.

3. Commit to fasting whatever you feel would be beneficial for you. You don't have to start with too much! This isn't meant to be a religious exercise but rather an action performed out of a longing for more of God. Ask the Spirit to see you through this process. Ask him to strengthen you as you become weak.

Nineteenth-century author Andrew Murray once said, "Prayer is reaching out after the unseen; fasting is letting go of all that is seen and temporal. Fasting helps express, deepen, confirm the resolution that we are ready to sacrifice anything, even ourselves to attain what we seek for the kingdom of God." May you discover the wealth of goodness that accompanies letting go of the weight of this world through fasting. And may your resolve to experience all that God has for you increase, as the cares of the world slip away.

Extended Reading: Acts 13

Seeking God through His Creation

DEVOTIONAL

Every part of creation, from the smallest of insects to the mountains in all their grandeur, proclaims the unspoken glory of God. Every living creature, rock, grain of sand, and mountain stream was created for a specific purpose. In the lilies of the field and the birds of the air, we discover God's faithfulness and

"You are the Lord, you alone. You have made heaven, the heaven of heavens, with all their host, the earth and all that is on it, the seas and all that is in them; and you preserve all of them; and the host of heaven worships you."

NEHEMIAH 9:6

provision (Matthew 6:28-30). With every sunrise we are reminded of Jesus' imminent return (Psalm 19:4-5). And with every gust of wind we are beckoned to live our lives as people of the Spirit (John 3:8).

Job 12:7-10 says, *"But ask the beasts, and they will teach you; the birds of the heavens, and they will tell you; or the bushes of the earth, and they will teach you; and the fish of the sea will declare to you. Who among all these does not know that the hand of the Lord has done this? In his hand is the life of every living thing and the breath of all mankind."* Are you allowing God to teach you through his creation? Are you taking in the unspeakable mystery and majesty found in the work of God's hands? Or are you merely passing by these beautiful, intentional poems written on the pages of leaves, blades, and dirt by the hand of your heavenly Father?

Psalm 19:1-4 says, *"The heavens declare the glory of God, and the sky above proclaims his handiwork. Day to day pours out speech, and night to night reveals knowledge. There is no speech, nor are there words, whose voice is not heard. Their voice goes out through all the*

earth, and their words to the end of the world." God is always speaking to you. Every piece of creation declares to you the depth of God's love, power, faithfulness, and nearness. Will you afford yourself the opportunity to stop and listen? Will you make space to open the eyes of your heart to receive the beauty, creativity, and love of your heavenly Father faithfully displayed before your very eyes?

To seek God without taking notice of his creation is to miss out on one of the most tangible and beautiful ways he speaks to us. It isn't too mystical or *"out there"* to ask God to show you his intent behind his creation. It's wholly Christian to spend time looking at and reflecting on the work of God's hands. Children of God across thousands of years have used creation to learn about their Creator. Scripture is filled with revelation received by God speaking through his creation. He has made everything as he did for a perfect and beneficial reason. May we be children who seek God through every avenue available to us. May we be believers who have the faith and patience to learn about our heavenly Father by the work of his hands.

63

GUIDED PRAYER

1. Meditate on God's desire to speak to you through his creation. Allow Scripture to renew your mind.

"But ask the beasts, and they will teach you; the birds of the heavens, and they will tell you; or the bushes of the earth, and they will teach you; and the fish of the sea will declare to you. Who among all these does not know that the hand of the Lord has done this? In his hand is the life of every living thing and the breath of all mankind." Job 12:7-10

"The heavens declare the glory of God, and the sky above proclaims his handiwork. Day to day pours out speech, and night to night reveals knowledge. There is no speech, nor are there words, whose voice is not heard. Their voice goes out through all the earth, and their words to the end of the world. In them he has set a tent for the sun, which comes out like a bridegroom leaving his chamber, and, like a strong man, runs its course with joy. Its rising is from the end of the heavens, and its circuit to the end of them, and there is nothing hidden from its heat." Psalm 19:1-6

2. Take some time to reflect on creation around you. It could be a flower, water, animal, or whatever you see.

"You are the Lord, you alone. You have made heaven, the heaven of heavens, with all their host, the earth and all that is on it, the seas and all that is in them; and you preserve all of them; and the host of heaven worships you." Nehemiah 9:6

3. Now ask God to teach you about his creation. What does he want to reveal about you and or himself?

"When I look at your heavens, the work of your fingers, the moon and the stars, which you have set in place, what is man that you are mindful of him, and the son of man that you care for him?" Psalm 8:3-4

A. W. Tozer said, "God dwells in His creation and is everywhere indivisibly present in all His works. He is transcendent above all His works even while He is immanent within them." May you go about your day with the knowledge that God is near to you. May creation declare to you the limitless love of your heavenly Father.

Extended Reading: Psalm 104

Seeking God in Solitude

DAY 13

DEVOTIONAL

Our world is filled with hustle and bustle. We reward busyness as if always working, striving, and achieving were the true marks of a life well-lived. We elevate those who have given everything to gain success. To be tired is to be weak. To be in need is to fail. To rest instead of work is to be lazy or selfish. As believers, we're living in a society whose values do not match that of our heavenly Father's. We need an adjustment of perspective.

"And after he had dismissed the crowds, he went up on the mountain by himself to pray. When evening came, he was there alone."

MATTHEW 14:23

We are created for time spent alone with our heavenly Father, away from the cares and ways of the world. We are created to seek God in solitude. Jesus modeled this important principle throughout his ministry. Luke 5:15-16 says, *"But now even more the report about him went abroad, and great crowds gathered to hear him and to be healed of their infirmities. But he would withdraw to desolate places and pray."* Mark 1:35 says, *"And rising very early in the morning, while it was still dark, he departed and went out to a desolate place, and there he prayed."* And Matthew 14:23 says, *"And after he had dismissed the crowds, he went up on the mountain by himself to pray. When evening came, he was there alone."* If Jesus needed time alone with the Father, you and I most certainly do.

Solitude is vital in our pursuit of deeper relationship with our heavenly Father. What would a marriage be if the couple only ever saw each other in large groups? What would a friendship be if you never spent time as just the two of you? Yet countless believers, Sunday after Sunday, file through church doors to meet with a God they are not encountering in the secret place. Our heavenly Father loves corporate worship to be sure, but community is intended to be an extension of the love and transformation we are receiving in solitude with God. Matthew 6:6 says, *"But when you pray, go into your room and shut the door and pray to your Father who is in secret. And your Father who sees in secret will reward you."* It's in the secret place that we learn what our Father is really like. It's in the secret place that we discern what his voice sounds like, find his heartbeat, and become like him.

Without solitude our faith will not stretch into the inner places of our hearts that so desperately need to be flooded with the light of glorious relationship with our heavenly Father. If you long to be loved, it's in the secret place you'll discover the wellspring of affections found in the heart of God. If you need someone to listen, it's in solitude you'll discover the always listening ear of your heavenly Father. And if you need a friend, it's in time spent alone fellowshipping with the Holy Spirit that you will find a friend who will never leave you, forsake you, hurt you, or mislead you.

May you discover what you've been longing for in the secret place with God. May you pursue deeper connection with your heavenly Father through the wonderful discipline of solitude.

GUIDED PRAYER

1. Meditate on God's desire to meet with you in the secret place.

"But when you pray, go into your room and shut the door and pray to your Father who is in secret. And your Father who sees in secret will reward you." Matthew 6:6

2. Reflect on your need for solitude. If Jesus needed time with the Father, receive the truth that you need it as well.

"And rising very early in the morning, while it was still dark, he departed and went out to a desolate place, and there he prayed." Mark 1:35

"But now even more the report about him went abroad, and great crowds gathered to hear him and to be healed of their infirmities. But he would withdraw to desolate places and pray." Luke 5:15-16

"And after he had dismissed the crowds, he went up on the mountain by himself to pray. When evening came, he was there alone." Matthew 14:23

3. Spend time alone pursuing God in solitude. Allow the silence to draw you into a deeper place of reflection. What has been hurting you? Where do you need your heavenly Father's affections?

"But when he who had set me apart before I was born, and who called me by his grace, was pleased to reveal his Son to me, in order that I might preach him among the Gentiles, I did not immediately consult with anyone; nor did I go up to Jerusalem to those who were apostles before me, but I went away into Arabia, and returned again to Damascus." Galatians 1:15-17

St. Anselm of Canterbury wrote, "Enter into the inner chamber of your mind. Shut out all things save God and whatever may aid you in seeking God; and having barred the door of your chamber, seek him." May you find the everlasting love of God as you seek him in solitude.

Extended Reading: Matthew 4

Seeking God through Community

DAY 14

DEVOTIONAL

We were not created to go about this life apart from relationship with fellow children of God. Without our brothers and sisters, we will never experience the fullness of life God intends for us. In community, we discover our place in the body of Christ. In community, we learn what it is to serve

"And let us consider how to stir up one another to love and good works, not neglecting to meet together, as is the habit of some, but encouraging one another, and all the more as you see the Day drawing near."

HEBREWS 10:24-25

out of love, honor, and respect. And in community, we receive the healing and love that can only come from those who share in the same Spirit.

Acts 2:42-47 says,

And they devoted themselves to the apostles' teaching and the fellowship, to the breaking of bread and the prayers. And awe came upon every soul, and many wonders and signs were being done through the apostles. And all who believed were together and had all things in common. And they were selling their possessions and belongings and distributing the proceeds to all, as any had need. And day by day, attending the temple together and breaking bread in their homes, they received their food with glad and generous hearts, praising God and having favor with all the people. And the Lord added to their number day by day those who were being saved.

Acts 2 describes community that my soul longs for. We were made for honest, vulnerable fellowship. We were created to help each other, eat together, worship our God, and love others. Through engaging with fellow believers, we become a witness to the world of what happens when God works in the hearts of his children. We declare through our love for each other the life and joy that comes from relationship with our heavenly Father.

Scripture is clear that true community requires sacrifice and vulnerability. 1 Corinthians 12:25-26 says, *"That there may be no division in the body, but that the members may have the same care for one another. If one member suffers, all suffer together; if one member is honored, all rejoice together."* God's desire is for all his children to humble themselves and live as one body. When one part of a physical body hurts, the rest of the body feels the pain and works together to heal. God desires it to be the same among the spiritual body of believers. He desires to fill us with his love and use us to provide healing for one another. He longs to guide us to a lifestyle of humility and sacrifice in pursuit of being his hands and feet for each other.

It takes receiving the love of God to give love. It requires a work of the Spirit to fill us with courage to be vulnerable with our community in order to receive and give the love we've been given in Christ. So, will you be a child filled with the love of your Father today? Will you allow God to use you to help a brother or sister? Will you choose the purpose and joy that comes from living sacrificially and vulnerably? If so, you will discover a satisfaction only found in the edification that comes from believers loving one another. May you find the fellowship your heart longs for as you courageously love your brothers and sisters.

71

GUIDED PRAYER

1. Meditate on the importance of community. Allow Scripture to fill you with a desire to love and be loved by your community.

"Two are better than one, because they have a good reward for their toil. For if they fall, one will lift up his fellow. But woe to him who is alone when he falls and has not another to lift him up! Again, if two lie together, they keep warm, but how can one keep warm alone? And though a man might prevail against one who is alone, two will withstand him—a threefold cord is not quickly broken." Ecclesiastes 4:9-12

"Iron sharpens iron, and one man sharpens another." Proverbs 27:17

"And they devoted themselves to the apostles' teaching and the fellowship, to the breaking of bread and the prayers. And awe came upon every soul, and many wonders and signs were being done through the apostles. And all who believed were together and had all things in common. And they were selling their possessions and belongings and distributing the proceeds to all, as any had need. And day by day, attending the temple together and breaking bread in their homes, they received their food with glad and generous hearts, praising God and having favor with all the people. And the Lord added to their number day by day those who were being saved." Acts 2:42-47

2. Reflect on your need for community. Where do you need the healing that comes from relationship with others? What people has God placed in your life? How can you in humility reach out to them for help?

3. Take time and pray for an increase in God-filled community in your life. How does he want to use you to help another person today? How can you lead out in being courageously vulnerable? If you lack such a thing, ask God to provide you with this type of community to share life with.

"Is anyone among you sick? Let him call for the elders of the church, and let them pray over him, anointing him with oil in the name of the Lord. And the prayer of faith will save the one who is sick, and the Lord will raise him up. And if he has committed sins, he will be forgiven. Therefore, confess your sins to one another and pray for one another, that you may be healed. The prayer of a righteous person has great power as it is working . . . My brothers, if anyone among you wanders from the truth and someone brings him back, let him know that whoever brings back a sinner from his wandering will save his soul from death and will cover a multitude of sins" James 5:13-16, 19-20

God doesn't ask us to wait for others to step out and live in accordance with his Spirit before he calls us too. His will for us doesn't hinge upon others' obedience. God is calling you to a lifestyle of joyful service, sacrifice, and love regardless of people's initiatives or responses. He longs to fill you with the courage to love others well and help them through their brokenness to a place of honesty and vulnerability. May you be the loving hands and feet of Jesus to your brothers and sisters who so desperately need a touch from God.

Extended Reading: Philippians 2

Joy

"Though you have not seen him, you love him. Though you do not now see him, you believe in him and rejoice with joy that is inexpressible and filled with glory." –1 Peter 1:8

WEEKLY OVERVIEW

As children of the Most High God, we are to be marked by contagious, unceasing joy. Through the Holy Spirit we have access to an unending supply of joy that comes from the wellspring of restored relationship with our heavenly Father. God longs to fill us with his joy that we might live the abundant life Jesus died to give us. He longs to make us children fashioned in the image of our Father that we might share his unending joy to a world without hope. May you discover the greater portion of joy available to you through the Spirit as you encounter the heart of your Father this week.

Strength in Joy

DEVOTIONAL

The strength that comes from the joy of restored relationship with our heavenly Father is unlike any other strength we can find in ourselves. The joy of the Lord is unceasing, unwavering, and powerful. It comes from a place of internal peace with God rather than external, fleeting circumstances. And it is wholly available to us through the sacrifice of Jesus Christ our Lord. May we be a people marked by the joy of our heavenly Father as we allow God to come and fill our lives with his powerful presence today.

*"And do not be grieved, for the joy
of the Lord is your strength."*

NEHEMIAH 8:10

Nehemiah 8 gives revelation on God's desire to establish joy at the foundation of following him. In Nehemiah 8, the nation of Israel had just rebuilt the walls around Jerusalem and were learning again what it is to live in obedience to the word of God. As Ezra opens God's word, the people fall on their faces in mourning and shame for their disobedience. And in response to their tears, Nehemiah proclaims to God's people, *"Eat the fat and drink sweet wine and send portions to anyone who has nothing ready, for this day is holy to our Lord. And do not be grieved, for the joy of the Lord is your strength"* (Nehemiah 8:10). God desires for joy to be at the foundation of relationship with him. He longs for us to be a people marked by the joy that can only come from restored relationship with our Creator. His joy is to be our strength.

The true picture of strength in the earth is total joy that comes from dependence on our heavenly Father. Psalm 16:8-11 says, *"I have set the Lord always before me; because he is at my right hand, I shall not be shaken.*

Therefore my heart is glad, and my whole being rejoices; my flesh also dwells secure. For you will not abandon my soul to Sheol, or let your holy one see corruption. You make known to me the path of life; in your presence there is fullness of joy; at your right hand are pleasures forevermore." It's only in utter dependence that the Lord is able to fully work in and through us. It's only in setting him always before us that we will be fully strengthened by the joy that comes from relationship with him. And it's only in continually seeking his presence that we will discover the fullness of joy and pleasure meant to be our portion as his children.

God wants to be your strength today. He wants to root and ground you in his unshakable joy. He longs to guide you to the still waters and do a mighty work in your heart to increase your capacity for his joy. Proverbs 17:22 says, *"A joyful heart is good medicine, but a crushed spirit dries up the bones."* May you discover the powerful medicine of joy today as you enter into a time of guided prayer.

GUIDED PRAYER

1. Meditate on the strength that comes from joy alone.
Allow Scripture to fill you with a desire to have more of the joy available to you in God.

"For the kingdom of God is not a matter of eating and drinking but of righteousness and peace and joy in the Holy Spirit."
Romans 14:17

"Go your way. Eat the fat and drink sweet wine and send portions to anyone who has nothing ready, for this day is holy to our Lord. And do not be grieved, for the joy of the LORD is your strength."
Nehemiah 8:10

"I have set the Lord always before me; because he is at my right hand, I shall not be shaken. Therefore my heart is glad, and my whole being rejoices; my flesh also dwells secure. For you will not abandon my soul to Sheol, or let your holy one see corruption. You make known to me the path of life; in your presence there is fullness of joy; at your right hand are pleasures forevermore." Psalm 16:8-11

2. What care, thought, or burden is keeping you from the fullness of joy today? What area of your life do you need to surrender in order to live in total dependence on your heavenly Father? Where is God wanting to fill you with his abundant joy today?

"A joyful heart is good medicine, but a crushed spirit dries up the bones." Proverbs 17:22

3. Surrender every area of your life to the capable hands of God and enter into the joy that comes from dependent relationship with your Creator. Rest in his peaceful presence and allow him to fill you with joy overflowing. Ask him to guide you into a more joyful life and to free you from whatever bonds would keep you from experiencing all he has for you.

"The Lord is my strength and my shield; in him my heart trusts, and I am helped; my heart exults, and with my song I give thanks to him." Psalm 28:7

"For you shall go out in joy and be led forth in peace; the mountains and the hills before you shall break forth into singing, and all the trees of the field shall clap their hands." Isaiah 55:12

May Paul's prayer to the Colossians be your pursuit today as you seek to live in the fullness of life Jesus died to give you:

"May you be strengthened with all power, according to his glorious might, for all endurance and patience with joy." Colossians 1:11

Extended Reading: Nehemiah 8

God Rejoices Over Us

DEVOTIONAL

Zephaniah 3:17 provides a constant source of joy by revealing insight into the heart of our loving, present heavenly Father. That scripture says, *"The Lord your God is in your midst, a mighty one who will save; he will rejoice over you with gladness; he will quiet you by his love; he will exult over you with loud singing."* As we look at this verse today, I pray that you will be filled with an abundant joy that can only come from a fresh, tangible revelation of your heavenly Father's overwhelming love for you.

"The Lord your God is in your midst." You can have joy today because your God is totally and powerfully present right where you are. Scripture says that he will never leave you or forsake you (Deuteronomy 31:6), his presence will go with you to the ends of the earth (Psalm 139:7-12), and at salvation you were made into a temple for the Holy Spirit (1 Corinthians 6:19). You can have joy because you are not alone in anything you do. God longs to make his presence known to you in every area of your life. He longs to do life with you—equipping you to live with total joy by filling you with his love every minute of every day.

"The Lord your God is . . . a mighty one who will save." You can have joy because you have been totally redeemed from the destitution of the world that surrounds you. You are saved from the perils of life without relationship with your Creator. You have been offered to spend eternity with the God of love who laid down his own life for yours. Your God has done a mighty work. You are now his child, healed and set free through the life, death, and resurrection of Jesus.

"He will rejoice over you with gladness." You can have joy because your God rejoices over you. You are not a failure in his eyes. He loves who you are. He is wholeheartedly glad you are his. He longs to fill you with the knowledge of his gladness today. He longs

to give you a revelation of how deeply in love with you he is. The Creator and Sustainer of all rejoices over you as his creation. You are not a mistake. You were made intentionally because your God longed to have relationship with you.

"He will quiet you by his love." You can have joy because your God will shepherd you to the still waters. His love will guide you to quiet places where your heart can be at rest. He will calm the areas of your life that are burdened and stressed by freeing you with the depths of his affections. You can have peace today in the presence of your heavenly Father no matter what situation you find yourself in. Your God will *"quiet you by his love"* as you follow the leadership of his Spirit.

"He will exult over you with loud singing." To exult is to be joyful or jubilant because of a triumph or success. You can have joy today because your God sees you as a triumph. You have been transformed. You are a new creation. You are what God has most desired in the earth. His chief longing has always been relationship with us, and by your faith in Jesus Christ you have given him what he has always wanted. God exults over you today just as you are. He longs for intimate relationship with you. He wants to give you ears to hear his *"loud singing"* that you might have the same perspective for yourself as he has for you.

In *The Ragamuffin Gospel*, Brennan Manning says, "My deepest awareness of myself is that I am deeply loved by Jesus Christ and I have done nothing to earn it or deserve it." May you come to the awareness of how deeply you are loved by your God today. May you allow God to love what you have deemed unlovable in your own life. And may Zephaniah 3:17 be a foundation on which you experience the overwhelming joy that comes from God's inexplicable love for you.

GUIDED PRAYER

1. Meditate on Zephaniah 3:17. Ask the Holy Spirit to highlight a part of the verse that you especially need today. Take time to allow Scripture to lay a foundation of truth on which you can have abundant joy.

"The Lord your God is in your midst, a mighty one who will save; he will rejoice over you with gladness; he will quiet you by his love; he will exult over you with loud singing." Zephaniah 3:17

2. Ask the Lord to reveal his nearness. Rest in his presence and allow his love to quiet and flood the weary places in your heart.

"For as a young man marries a young woman, so shall your sons marry you, and as the bridegroom rejoices over the bride, so shall your God rejoice over you." Isaiah 62:5

3. Ask the Holy Spirit to fill you with abundant joy for today. Ask him to teach you how to live a joyful lifestyle where you experience the fruit of his presence through any circumstance.

"The Lord takes pleasure in those who fear him, in those who hope in his steadfast love." Psalm 147:11

In Scripture, we have a source of constancy and steadfastness for our emotions. If we will allow Scripture to be the basis on which we think and feel, we can experience a joy that is unshakable by the passing tides of circumstance. Scriptures like Zephaniah 3:17 are vital to a healthy emotional life. We need constant reminders of the truth so that we can base our emotions on who God is rather than what is going on with the world around us. May you enter into a new season of abundant joy as you allow God's word to be your emotional source and guide.

Extended Reading: Zephaniah 3

The Fullness of Joy

DAY 17

DEVOTIONAL

By the grace of God, we have a beautiful inheritance of eternal and tangible relationship with our heavenly Father. Psalm 16:5-6 says, *"The Lord is my chosen portion and my cup; you hold my lot. The lines have fallen for me in pleasant places; indeed, I have a beautiful inheritance."* And later in verse 11 David

"You make known to me the path of life; in your presence there is fullness of joy; at your right hand are pleasures forevermore."

PSALM 16:11

writes, *"You make known to me the path of life; in your presence there is fullness of joy; at your right hand are pleasures forevermore."*

God has designated the beautiful inheritance of his presence for us. Israel knew what it was to center their gatherings around the presence of God. His presence guided them through the wilderness. His presence won battles for them. His presence was powerful in the Holy of Holies. God's presence was the sign that he was with them and for them.

And Psalm 16:11 tells us that in the presence of God *"there is fullness of joy."* Imagine what the fullness of joy looks and feels like. What would it be like to have a real encounter with the fullness of joy today? In the fullness of joy there is no sorrow, worry, doubt, or fear. In the fullness of joy there is abundant life, peace, freedom, and love.

Psalm 43:4 says, *"Then I will go to the altar of God, to God my exceeding joy."* Consistently encountering the presence of our heavenly Father is the sole source of *"exceeding joy"* on this earth. Only in spending time

going to his altar will we experience the joy that is our portion. Only in his presence will the joy of the Lord truly become our strength (Nehemiah 8:10).

Heavenly joy is an essential element to the Christian life. Joy isn't something we are created to live without. It isn't a pursuit secondary to other pursuits. Heavenly joy is a cornerstone on which we live lives that reflect the goodness, grace, love, and reality of our heavenly Father. Joy is meant to be the mouthpiece by which we declare how wonderful a relationship with God truly is.

In his book *In Our Joy*, John Piper writes, "But when God gives the radical change of new birth and repentance, Jesus himself becomes our supreme treasure." Choose the better portion today of spending time encountering the fullness of joy that can only be found in the presence of God. Allow God to bring a radical change of new birth and repentance that positions Christ as your supreme treasure. And pursue heavenly joy today that you might demonstrate the surpassing kindness of your heavenly Father to a world that is desperately seeking what can only be found in restored relationship with him.

GUIDED PRAYER

1. Meditate on the fullness of joy available in the presence of God. Allow Scripture to stir up a desire to encounter the joy of the Lord today.

"You make known to me the path of life; in your presence there is fullness of joy; at your right hand are pleasures forevermore." Psalm 16:11

"Then I will go to the altar of God, to God my exceeding joy." Psalm 43:4

"The Lord is my chosen portion and my cup; you hold my lot. The lines have fallen for me in pleasant places; indeed, I have a beautiful inheritance." Psalm 16:5-6

2. Ask the Lord to reveal his nearness. God is never far from you. His presence is with you. He longs to make himself known. Simply rest in the truth of his nearness and allow him to reveal himself to you.

"Even the sparrow finds a home, and the swallow a nest for herself, where she may lay her young, at your altars, O Lord of hosts, my King and my God." Psalm 84:3

3. Ask God to guide you into the fullness of joy available in his presence. Ask him to fill you with abundant joy that you might live today declaring his goodness to the world around you.

"The thief comes only to steal and kill and destroy. I came that they may have life and have it abundantly." John 10:10

"But now I am coming to you, and these things I speak in the world, that they may have my joy fulfilled in themselves." John 17:13

"These things I have spoken to you, that my joy may be in you, and that your joy may be full." John 15:11

I pray that as the bride of Christ we would grow in our knowledge of his nearness. I pray that we would walk in the fullness of relationship with our heavenly Father available to us on the earth. And I pray that we would grow in our reflection of God's goodness to a world that longs to know him. May you pursue the presence of God with greater fervor as you go throughout your day. May you experience his nearness and live your life with the joy of the Lord as your strength.

Extended Reading: Psalm 16

Joy in Every Circumstance

DEVOTIONAL

The joy of the Lord available to us in the Holy Spirit transcends all circumstances, relationships, and possessions. It is an internal joy fed to our hearts by the wellspring of joy the Father has toward us. God longs to make us a people marked by his joy. He longs to fill us with the knowledge of how thrilled he is to be our Father. He longs to make us a joyful people in every circumstance and season. 1 Peter 1:6-9 says,

*"Those who sow in tears shall reap with shouts
of joy! He who goes out weeping, bearing the
seed for sowing, shall come home with shouts of
joy, bringing his sheaves with him."*

PSALM 126:5-6

"In this you rejoice, though now for a little while, if necessary, you have been grieved by various trials, so that the tested genuineness of your faith—more precious than gold that perishes though it is tested by fire—may be found to result in praise and glory and honor at the revelation of Jesus Christ. Though you have not seen him, you love him. Though you do not now see him, you believe in him and rejoice with joy that is inexpressible and filled with glory, obtaining the outcome of your faith, the salvation of your souls."

We can have joy in the midst of trial and tribulation because we have a genuine faith that this life is not all there is. Our hope reaches far beyond the confines of this fleeting age of sin and separation from God and looks toward the day when we will live in perfect, face-to-face relationship with our Creator. Every trial and tribulation is an opportunity to cling to the truth that this world is not our home and to be filled with joy at the thought of what awaits us on the other side of this life.

James 1:2-4 says, *"Count it all joy, my brothers, when you meet trials of various kinds, for you know that the testing of your faith produces steadfastness. And let*

steadfastness have its full effect, that you may be perfect and complete, lacking in nothing." While God may not cause the various trials we face, he most certainly uses them to cause our joy to find its source in him alone. Our heavenly Father knows that if we place our joy in the fleeting and fickle circumstances of this life our lives will be an emotional rollercoaster rather than a reflection of how consistently good he is.

Your heavenly Father has a compassionate heart toward the problems you face. He never desires for you to act or try and drum up faith that everything will be all right. He longs to meet you at the very core of your trial and fill you with abundant joy that's rooted in his love alone. He longs to guide you through the tough seasons of life that try and rob you of your allotted portion of joy. He longs to make your faith steadfast and sure so you can meet the tribulations of this world head-on with joy. Run to your Father today with every weight and problem. Ask him to guide you to the still waters that your soul might be restored. And receive all the joy he longs to give you today as you encounter his deep and powerful love for you.

GUIDED PRAYER

1. Meditate on God's desire to fill you with joy in every circumstance.

"Those who sow in tears shall reap with shouts of joy! He who goes out weeping, bearing the seed for sowing, shall come home with shouts of joy, bringing his sheaves with him." Psalm 126:5-6

"Count it all joy, my brothers, when you meet trials of various kinds, for you know that the testing of your faith produces steadfastness. And let steadfastness have its full effect, that you may be perfect and complete, lacking in nothing." James 1:2-4

2. What trial or tribulation are you facing that God longs to use to strengthen your faith with joy? Where does God want to meet you today that you might live with the joy of his love rather than the weight of the world?

3. Ask God to guide you to the source of joy for your circumstance. Ask the Holy Spirit to give you proper perspective about your life. Open your heart and allow God to come and love you where you're at.

"Restore to me the joy of your salvation, and uphold me with a willing spirit." Psalm 51:12

May Mother Teresa's words spur you toward a lifestyle of joy today:

"Joy is prayer – Joy is strength – Joy is love – Joy is a net of love by which you can catch souls. God loves a cheerful giver. She gives most who gives with joy. The best way to show our gratitude to God and the people is to accept everything with joy. A joyful heart is the inevitable result of a heart burning with love. Never let anything so fill you with sorrow as to make you forget the joy of the Christ risen."

Extended Reading: James 1

Joy from the Spirit

DEVOTIONAL

Relationship with the Holy Spirit empowers us to live a lifestyle of consistent joy. It's only by the filling of the Spirit that we have access to the deep reservoirs of joy found in the heart of our heavenly Father. Galatians 5:22 is clear that the fruit of the Spirit for believers is to be joy, so as temples of the Holy Spirit we need to search out what it looks like to allow the fruit of joy to be evident in our hearts and lives.

Scripture is filled with direct connections between the filling of the Holy Spirit and joy. Romans 14:17 says, *"For the kingdom of God is not a matter of eating and drinking but of righteousness and peace and joy in the Holy Spirit."* Acts 13:52 says, *"And the disciples were filled with joy and with the Holy Spirit."* 1 Thessalonians 1:6-7 says, *"And you became imitators of us and of the Lord, for you received the word in much affliction, with the joy of the Holy Spirit, so that you became an example to all the believers in Macedonia and in Achaia."*

We are not designed to have joy in ourselves. Rather, such joy comes by the dwelling of the Holy Spirit within us. As the disciples began to be filled with the Holy Spirit, their lives changed dramatically. They went from fearful, fair-weathered followers of Jesus to joy-filled, sacrificial, and empowered world changers. They had joy in the midst of intense persecution because they had the Holy Spirit filling them with the fruits of his indwelling.

We have the same Holy Spirit the disciples had, and he longs to do the same kind of works in you and me today as he did in them thousands of years ago.

He longs to fill us with joy in the midst of any trial or pain. He longs to heal and transform our hearts into greater reflections of God's goodness. He longs to make us a people so joyful that there is no other explanation for our joy other than God is with us.

So, how do we allow the Spirit to bear the fruit of joy in our lives? How do we grow in our relationship with this mysterious part of the Godhead? It all starts with a posture of humility and prayer. The Holy Spirit never forces us into deeper relationship with him. He is peaceful, powerful, loving, and patient. You must make time to respond to his small tugs on your heart in order to walk in greater relationship with him. You must humble yourself and ask for more of him, whatever that looks like. Allow the truth of God's love

and faithfulness to cast out any fear or reservation about a lifestyle of total connection with the Holy Spirit. Ask him to fill you to overflowing today and guide you to a lifestyle of bearing the fruit of intimate relationship with him.

The Spirit knows how to guide our hearts. He knows if we were made more introverted or extroverted. He knows if we were made more intuitive, pragmatic, or logical. And he knows the perfect ways to guide us into deeper, more fruitful lives. Spend time allowing the Spirit to lead you into a life filled with more joy. Allow him to speak to you and lead you in whatever ways he desires. And rest in his loving presence as you learn what it is to reach greater depths of relationship with him.

GUIDED PRAYER

1. Meditate on the importance of relationship with the Holy Spirit in having joy. Allow Scripture to stir up your desire for deeper intimacy with the Spirit.

"But the fruit of the Spirit is love, joy, peace, patience, kindness, goodness, faithfulness, gentleness, self-control; against such things there is no law." Galatians 5:22-23

"For the kingdom of God is not a matter of eating and drinking but of righteousness and peace and joy in the Holy Spirit." Romans 14:17

"And the disciples were filled with joy and with the Holy Spirit." Acts 13:52

2. Ask the Holy Spirit to reveal his nearness. Ask him to help you become more aware of his presence in your life.

3. Ask the Holy Spirit to guide you to greater depths of joy. Ask him to bear the fruit of joy in your life throughout any and every circumstance. Spend time allowing him to show you what might be in your way and the portion of joy afforded to you by his dwelling within you.

The absolute best way we can live is in total and complete surrender to the Holy Spirit. When we allow him to take the reins of our lives, he guides us to far greener and more abundant pastures than we could ever find ourselves. He has the ability and desire to lead us into the fullness of God's plans for our lives, but we must be willing to follow him wherever he would lead us. Follow his direction today. Look for his guidance. And walk into a life filled with the joy of the Holy Spirit.

Extended Reading: Romans 8

Inexpressible Joy

DEVOTIONAL

1 Peter 1:8-9 fills my heart with a longing to rejoice in ways that move the heart of my heavenly Father. That scripture says, *"Though you have not seen him, you love him. Though you do not now see him, you believe in him and rejoice with joy that is inexpressible and filled with glory, obtaining the outcome of your faith, the salvation of your souls."* What does it look like to rejoice with joy that is *"inexpressible and filled with glory?"* What would it be like to have our hearts so filled with praise that our lips can't articulate the overwhelming goodness of God?

"Though you have not seen him, you love him. Though you do not now see him, you believe in him and rejoice with joy that is inexpressible and filled with glory, obtaining the outcome of your faith, the salvation of your souls."

1 PETER 1:8-9

In the famous hymn, *The Love of God*, Frederick M. Lehman wrote, "The love of God is greater far than tongue or pen can ever tell; it goes beyond the highest star, and reaches to the lowest hell." We are designed to be continually awed by the wondrous works of our heavenly Father. So great is his love for us that all the ink and paper in the world couldn't adequately describe the depths of his mercies toward his children. So infinite is his nature that the fastest vessel could never reach the ends of his heart. And so powerful is his affection that we as his children will never be able to stop singing his praise.

Do you feel awed by God today? Is your heart wrapped up in the unfathomable goodness of his grace? Being filled with inexpressible joy is the natural response to seeing how truly good God is in comparison to how truly broken we are. Joy is meant to be the overflow of true, tangible relationship with a God who would lay down his own life solely because he desperately longed for restored relationship with us.

As children of the Most High God, we must take time to allow him to awe us. We must take time to wonder at his amazing works. We are created with an insatiable longing for fascination. We love to ponder on that which we will never fully comprehend. God created the universe as an example of how unfathomable and fascinating he is. Proverbs 25:2 says, *"It is the glory of God to conceal things, but the glory of kings is to search things out."* He is a God full of wonderful mystery we were designed to search out. It is our inexpressible joy to spend time with the Creator of galaxies that the human eye will never see and minute details too small to ever behold.

Matthew 13:44 says, *"The kingdom of heaven is like treasure hidden in a field, which a man found and covered up. Then in his joy he goes and sells all that he has and buys that field."* God is worth your life. The fullness of relationship with him is far greater than any possession man could ever attain. The great mystery in all of creation is a mere reflection of the infinite, loving nature of our heavenly Father. Take time today to devote yourself to rejoicing with inexpressible joy at the revelation of how great God is. Allow him to guide you into new and refreshing depths of his love. May you discover today the treasure of restored relationship with your mysterious and fascinating heavenly Father.

101

GUIDED PRAYER

1. Meditate on the infinite and wonderful nature of God. Think about his creation and how all of it was created by his word. Reflect on the powerful and loving sacrifice of Jesus. Allow Scripture and the divine nature of God to fill you with fascination and inexpressible joy.

"For his invisible attributes, namely, his eternal power and divine nature, have been clearly perceived, ever since the creation of the world, in the things that have been made." Romans 1:20

"But he was wounded for our transgressions; he was crushed for our iniquities; upon him was the chastisement that brought us peace, and with his stripes we are healed." Isaiah 53:5

"Before the mountains were brought forth, or ever you had formed the earth and the world, from everlasting to everlasting you are God." Psalm 90:2

2. Ask God to guide you into new depths of his heart today. Ask him to show you something about himself you didn't know. Ask the Holy Spirit to teach you how to search out the incredible mysteries of God.

3. Spend time resting in the presence of your Creator. The Creator of the entire universe is with you right now. The God who formed every mountain, star, and grain of sand loves you and longs to be with you. Allow the incredible goodness of God to overwhelm the tired and dry places of your heart.

Psalm 63:1 says, *"O God, you are my God; earnestly I seek you; my soul thirsts for you; my flesh faints for you, as in a dry and weary land where there is no water."* May we be a people who earnestly seek God for the refreshment of our souls. May we discover the still waters of his presence that have the power to replenish that which the world has dried out. May we run to God when we have need, knowing that he is willing and able to supply everything we need and more. And may a fresh revelation of God's love fill you with inexpressible joy that resounds in everything you do today.

Extended Reading: Psalm 90

Being a
Carrier of Joy

DEVOTIONAL

As disciples of Jesus, we are to carry the joy of our salvation everywhere we go. You and I have the power to change atmospheres on earth with the joy of the Spirit. We have the power to brighten people's days, break off heaviness, and lead people to a deeper revelation of the goodness of our Lord when we reflect his joy to others.

*"For you shall go out in joy and be led forth
in peace; the mountains and the hills before you
shall break forth into singing, and all the trees of
the field shall clap their hands."*

ISAIAH 55:12

God is a joyful God. He is the inventor of happiness and fun. Luke 15:10 says, *"Just so, I tell you, there is joy before the angels of God over one sinner who repents."* Nehemiah 8:10 tells us *"the joy of the Lord is [our] strength."* In order to truly declare to the world who our heavenly Father is, we must be carriers of joy. We must be a people marked by the joy that only comes from restored relationship with an all-knowing, all-powerful, and all-loving God.

It's taken me a long time to learn and an even longer time to realize the truth that circumstances, people, trials, work, and worldly stress do not have the inherent ability to steal my joy. It's when I open my heart to outside elements that I allow stresses to come in like robbers and take what is rightfully mine in the Lord. It's when I allow a fellow driver, a time crunch, a negative comment, or a troublesome problem to take precedence over the joy and hope I have in Jesus that I step outside of my allotted portion of peace.

To be carriers of joy, we have to choose to value the fruit of the Spirit over worldly emotions. We have to choose to only open our hearts to the things of God

and shrug off that which is fleeting. If we don't take control of our thoughts and cast any fear, worry, or doubt on the shoulders of our heavenly Father, the circumstances of this world will rule our emotions rather than the steadfast joy of the Spirit.

Isaiah 55:12 says, *"For you shall go out in joy and be led forth in peace; the mountains and the hills before you shall break forth into singing, and all the trees of the field shall clap their hands."* The Lord longs to make us a people that go out in joy. He longs to make us children who are overwhelmed by his love to the degree that the cares of this world pale in comparison to his grace and affections. Ask the Lord for perspective today. Allow the Spirit to help you focus your attention on the true purpose for which you were created: restored relationship with your heavenly Father. Choose the joy of the Lord over the stress and cares of the world. Choose to *"be led forth in peace"* rather than led by your flesh. And experience today the lifestyle of carrying the joy of the Lord with you everywhere you go. May others come to know the abundant goodness of your heavenly Father through the way you exude joy.

105

GUIDED PRAYER

1. Meditate on the importance of carrying joy. Allow Scripture to establish a new emphasis on joy for you.

"A joyful heart is good medicine, but a crushed spirit dries up the bones." Proverbs 17:22

"For the kingdom of God is not a matter of eating and drinking but of righteousness and peace and joy in the Holy Spirit." Romans 14:17

"For you shall go out in joy and be led forth in peace; the mountains and the hills before you shall break forth into singing, and all the trees of the field shall clap their hands." Isaiah 55:12

2. What do you allow to steal your joy? What circumstances, negative comments, or people have been robbing you of peace? Ask the Holy Spirit to reveal the root of whatever is stealing your joy.

"The hope of the righteous brings joy, but the expectation of the wicked will perish." Proverbs 10:28

3. Surrender your emotions and thoughts to the Lord alone. Ask the Spirit to help you open your heart only to the things of him instead of the things of the world. Ask him to make you a carrier of joy.

"And you became imitators of us and of the Lord, for you received the word in much affliction, with the joy of the Holy Spirit, so that you became an example to all the believers in Macedonia and in Achaia." 1 Thessalonians 1:6-7

Our heavenly Father is much more patient than we often believe. He is not in a rush with you. He will not let you miss his perfect will for your life if you are willing to follow him in obedience. Trust in his timing. Cast off the burden of paving your own way to an impactful life. Take time to become a carrier of joy by resting in his presence and getting to know his heart. Allow his perspective of patience to become your perspective. May you be filled with peace and joy in the knowledge of your God's great love for you.

Extended Reading: Isaiah 55

Peace

WEEK

"*Peace I leave with you; my peace I give to you. Not as the world gives do I give to you.*"
–John 14:27

WEEKLY OVERVIEW

One of the most powerful marks on the life of a believer is transcendent peace. This world offers us no reason to be peaceful. It offers us no reason to be without stress, burdens, cares, and total frustration. But we serve a God who offers us peace in the midst of any circumstance. We serve a God in whom all true peace finds its source. May you discover the heart of your heavenly Father to bring you peace this week.

The Prince of Peace

DEVOTIONAL

We serve a God who is the author, giver, and sustainer of peace. Isaiah 9:6 prophesied about Christ by saying, *"For to us a child is born, to us a son is given; and the government shall be upon his shoulder, and his name shall be called Wonderful Counselor, Mighty God, Everlasting Father, Prince of Peace."* In order for us to fully grasp and live with the peace promised to us in Scripture, we must first understand the peaceful nature of our God.

"For to us a child is born, to us a son is given; and the government shall be upon his shoulder, and his name shall be called Wonderful Counselor, Mighty God, Everlasting Father, Prince of Peace."

ISAIAH 9:6

The pages of Scripture are filled with declarations about God's peaceful nature and desire for peace on the earth. 1 Corinthians 14:33 says, *"For God is not a God of confusion but of peace."* Romans 14:17 says, *"For the kingdom of God is not a matter of eating and drinking but of righteousness and peace and joy in the Holy Spirit."* And Philippians 4:9 says, *"What you have learned and received and heard and seen in me—practice these things, and the God of peace will be with you."*

God longs to bring us peace as his children. He longs to make us like himself in that we would have peace in the midst of any circumstance. Nothing robs God of his peace. Nothing can take it away. Peace is within the very nature of our Creator. And when we come to him, open our heart, and receive his presence we naturally become like him. Seeking true peace is synonymous with seeking the presence of God because he is peace.

2 Thessalonians 3:16 says, *"Now may the Lord of peace himself give you peace at all times in every way. The Lord be with you all."* What it takes for us to have peace *"at all times in every way"* is to simply fellowship with *"the Lord of peace."* When we meet with God we position ourselves to receive all the abundant life he has to give. In encountering a peaceful God the weight of the world seems to lift off. In discovering his unconditional love the stress of continually seeking love from others falls away.

We serve a God who has peace for us right now. We can cast all our cares and burdens on his shoulders. He can handle all the cares of the world because he is Lord of them all. Take time to meet with the God of peace today and receive the peace that surpasses all understanding.

GUIDED PRAYER

1. Meditate on the peaceful nature of God. Allow Scripture to reorient your understanding of who God is and how he feels about you.

"Now may the Lord of peace himself give you peace at all times in every way. The Lord be with you all." 2 Thessalonians 3:16

"For to us a child is born, to us a son is given; and the government shall be upon his shoulder, and his name shall be called Wonderful Counselor, Mighty God, Everlasting Father, Prince of Peace." Isaiah 9:6

2. Where are you without peace today? What situation, person, or concern is robbing you of peace?

3. Receive the presence of God and the peace that comes with encountering your heavenly Father's heart. Cast your cares on his shoulders and receive the peace that comes from trusting in the goodness, nearness, capability, and availability of God.

"Cast all your anxiety on him because he cares for you." 1 Peter 5:7 (NIV)

"I have said these things to you, that in me you may have peace. In the world you will have tribulation. But take heart; I have overcome the world." John 16:33

Oftentimes peace comes by choice. The things of this world affect us wrongly when we view them apart from a heavenly perspective. Paul writes in Philippians 3:8, *"Indeed, I count everything as loss because of the surpassing worth of knowing Christ Jesus my Lord. For his sake I have suffered the loss of all things and count them as rubbish, in order that I may gain Christ."* Don't allow the stresses of this life to rob you of a heavenly peace found in trusting God. Take heart that God will bring you peace and joy in the midst of any circumstance if you allow him to. May Romans 15:33 serve as a benediction and peaceful foundation for the rest of your day today: *"May the God of peace be with you all. Amen."*

Extended Reading: John 16

Peace is a Fruit

DAY 23

DEVOTIONAL

Living with true peace can only be done by allowing the Holy Spirit to bear the fruit of his presence in our lives. Galatians 5:23-23 says, *"But the fruit of the Spirit is love, joy, peace, patience, kindness, goodness, faithfulness, gentleness, self-control; against such things there is no law."* How

"But the fruit of the Spirit is love,
joy, peace, patience, kindness, goodness,
faithfulness, gentleness, self-control;
against such things there is no law."

GALATIANS 5:22-23

incredible is it that we can have peace in this world through relationship with the Holy Spirit! The fact that true peace is solely a fruit of the Spirit takes the weight of peace off our shoulders.

It's impossible to bear the fruit of peace apart from connectivity to God. It's impossible to force peace in our lives because it's impossible for us to bear fruit in our own strength. John 15:4 says, *"Abide in me, and I in you. As the branch cannot bear fruit by itself, unless it abides in the vine, neither can you, unless you abide in me."* Peace is the fruit of abiding in the Holy Spirit. It's the fruit of surrendering our perspectives, relationships, words, actions, thoughts, and emotions to him.

If we are living without peace, it is because we have yet to allow the Holy Spirit to fill an area of our life with his presence. If our thoughts aren't marked by the peace of God's truth, it's because we have

yet to allow the Spirit to renew our minds with the Scripture he authored. If we're without peace in our relationships, it's because we haven't allowed him to reveal to us his heart for ourselves or others. If the opinion of man continually robs us of peace, it's because we haven't centered our lives around his opinion of us. The list continues but the point remains the same. To live with peace is to allow the Spirit to permeate every area of life with his powerful, loving, and transformative presence.

Romans 14:17 says, *"For the kingdom of God is not a matter of eating and drinking but of righteousness and peace and joy in the Holy Spirit."* May you choose to seek the kingdom of God above all else today. May you allow the Holy Spirit to bring heaven to earth, not only in your life but everywhere you go today. Seek a greater measure of communion with the Holy Spirit today and enjoy the fruit of peace that comes from his nearness.

GUIDED PRAYER

1. Meditate on the nature of peace as a fruit of the Holy Spirit.

"But the fruit of the Spirit is love, joy, peace, patience, kindness, goodness, faithfulness." Galatians 5:22

2. Where is your life not marked by the fruit of the Spirit? Where is your life not filled with the peace of his presence?

3. Ask the Holy Spirit to guide you into a deeper level of communion with him today. Take time to receive an awareness of his nearness.

"And do not get drunk with wine, for that is debauchery, but be filled with the Spirit." Ephesians 5:18

"You, however, are not in the flesh but in the Spirit, if in fact the Spirit of God dwells in you." Romans 8:9

Growing in relationship with the Holy Spirit is like growing in relationship with anyone else. He is a person of the Trinity just like the Father and Jesus. It takes time to get to know someone. It takes effort to learn their wants, desires, and personality. If you pursue a deeper connection with the Spirit you will find it. May you grow in your awareness of your union with the Holy Spirit who dwells within you.

Extended Reading: Galatians 5

A Peaceful Thought-Life

DAY 24

DEVOTIONAL

Your thought-life can either be a place of peace and life or a source of immense internal struggle and despair. It's our thoughts that the enemy tries to affect with half-truths and outright lies. It's our thoughts that are the gateway to our emotions and actions.

*"For to set the mind on the flesh is death, but to
set the mind on the Spirit is life and peace."*

ROMANS 8:6

And it's our thoughts our loving heavenly Father longs to influence, redeem, and renew that we might experience everlasting peace.

Isaiah 26:3 says, *"You keep him in perfect peace whose mind is stayed on you, because he trusts in you."* Do you long for perfect peace today? Do you long to keep your mind stayed on the inexpressible excellencies of Jesus? It all starts with trust. When we allow our minds to stray into worry, doubt, fear, reservation, and lies, it is because we don't trust that God is who he says he is or that he will do what he says he'll do.

If we truly trusted God with our relationships, we wouldn't spend so much energy mulling over conversations that could have been better or different. If we truly trusted God as the perfect provider of our finances and possessions, we wouldn't spend so much time overwhelming ourselves with all the different financial opportunities available, or not available, to us. If we truly trusted God with our futures, we wouldn't devote so much of our minds to playing out every scenario that could possibly happen. And if we truly trusted God that we are loved, liked, enjoyable, and wholly found,

we wouldn't spend so much time thinking of ways we can impress others, work our way into a clique, make others laugh, or win the affections of another.

Romans 8:6 says, *"For to set the mind on the flesh is death, but to set the mind on the Spirit is life and peace."* Where you set your mind today is your decision. The Spirit is fully available, ready and willing to lead you to abounding joy and peace. And the enemy is prowling like a lion seeking to devour your thoughts that they might breed emotional and even physical death (1 Peter 5:8).

There is a battle for your thoughts happening every moment. But greater is he who is in you than he who is in the world (1 John 4:4). God has a perfect plan to lead you away from thoughts that plague you into life and joy in the Holy Spirit. Trust him as your good and loving Father. Trust that he is always with you. Place your faith wholeheartedly in him because he is perfectly faithful and able. He has plans for an incredible hope and future for you if you will simply trust him and set your mind on him as often and as passionately as you can. May you find peace today in your thoughts through a powerful revelation of God's abiding love.

123

GUIDED PRAYER

1. Meditate on the importance of placing your trust in God. Allow Scripture to stir up your desire to have a peaceful thought-life.

"You keep him in perfect peace whose mind is stayed on you, because he trusts in you." Isaiah 26:3

"Do not be conformed to this world, but be transformed by the renewal of your mind, that by testing you may discern what is the will of God, what is good and acceptable and perfect." Romans 12:2

"For to set the mind on the flesh is death, but to set the mind on the Spirit is life and peace." Romans 8:6

2. What thoughts plague you the most? What thoughts steal the peace available to you through trusting God?

"If then you have been raised with Christ, seek the things that are above, where Christ is, seated at the right hand of God. Set your minds on things that are above, not on things that are on earth." Colossians 3:1-2

3. Place your trust fully in God today for whatever specifically troubles you and receive the peace that comes from setting your mind on your good and loving heavenly Father.

"Trust in the Lord with all your heart, and do not lean on your own understanding." Proverbs 3:5

"Delight yourself in the Lord, and he will give you the desires of your heart. Commit your way to the Lord; trust in him, and he will act. He will bring forth your righteousness as the light, and your justice as the noonday." Psalm 37:4-6

"The Lord is my strength and my shield; in him my heart trusts, and I am helped; my heart exults, and with my song I give thanks to him." Psalm 28:7

Our thoughts truly are a powerful gauge of our level of trust. Thoughts don't run themselves. We think the way we do for a reason. When we begin to take captive and evaluate our thoughts, we embark on an important process of renewing our minds. Take notice of the way you think today. Take notice of what troubles you and what brings you peace and joy. Open your heart and ask the Holy Spirit to help you renew your mind and place your trust in him that you might truly have peace. May your thoughts be marked by the nearness and love of Jesus.

Extended Reading: Psalm 37

Peace in Relationships

DAY 25

DEVOTIONAL

Relationships are one of the parts of life that can most rob us of our peace in the Holy Spirit. Our lives are all in some way impacted by one another. If I am counting on someone and they don't come through, it can profoundly impact my circumstances. If I truly love someone and they wound, neglect, or reject me, it can undoubtedly hinder my ability to enjoy the peace of God. But God offers us peace in the midst of all circumstances. Jesus maintained peace

*"And let the peace of Christ rule in your hearts, to
which indeed you were called in one body."*

COLOSSIANS 3:15

in the Holy Spirit in the midst of those he loved shouting, *"Crucify him!"* (Luke 23:21). May God lead us today to a path of continual peace founded on his love and truth.

Colossians 3:12-15 describes a road map to powerful, transcendent peace in our relationships. Scripture says,

Put on then, as God's chosen ones, holy and beloved, compassionate hearts, kindness, humility, meekness, and patience, bearing with one another and, if one has a complaint against another, forgiving each other; as the Lord has forgiven you, so you also must forgive. And above all these put on love, which binds everything together in perfect harmony. And let the peace of Christ rule in your hearts, to which indeed you were called in one body. And be thankful.

The pathway to peace with others begins with choosing to die to yourself. We are completely unable to control anyone. Each person has a will and the power to love us or reject us. Even believers will consistently fail you. If the people of God could stand in the presence of God incarnate and shout, *"Crucify him,"* you can know others will reject you. But when you choose to continually

humble yourself before others and serve, you will be filled with the *"peace of Christ"* (Colossians 3:15). When we choose to put on *"compassionate hearts, kindness, humility, meekness, and patience"* regardless of the actions of others, we position ourselves to continually bear the fruit of peace (Colossians 3:12).

We find our greatest example of this in the person of Jesus. Just as he could ask forgiveness from his heavenly Father by saying, *"Father, forgive them, for they know not what they do,"* as the soldiers who nailed him to the cross gambled for his clothing, you will have a supernatural peace when you choose to live selflessly in love (Luke 23:24). The Holy Spirit will fill you with peace in your relationships when you choose to live like Jesus.

Take time today to put on a *"compassionate [heart], kindness, humility, meekness, and patience"* (Colossians 3:12). Choose to die to yourself and live for Christ. And watch as the Holy Spirit anoints you with the fruit of peace and love to live like Jesus did. May your relationships be filled with patience today as you live in obedience to the word of your loving heavenly Father.

127

GUIDED PRAYER

1. Meditate on Scripture's command to die to yourself and live like Jesus.

"If anyone would come after me, let him deny himself and take up his cross daily and follow me." Luke 9:23

"For whoever would save his life will lose it, but whoever loses his life for my sake and the gospel's will save it." Mark 8:35

"I have been crucified with Christ. It is no longer I who live, but Christ who lives in me. And the life I now live in the flesh I live by faith in the Son of God, who loved me and gave himself for me." Galatians 2:20

2. What would it be like to live in a consistent posture of love and humility rather than in response to the actions of others? What sort of peace would you feel if your emotions and actions were less founded on others and more based on the unconditional love and commands of God?

3. Choose to live today in humility and service. Decide to die to yourself and live in total surrender to the Holy Spirit.

"So if there is any encouragement in Christ, any comfort from love, any participation in the Spirit, any affection and sympathy, complete my joy by being of the same mind, having the same love, being in full accord and of one mind. Do nothing from rivalry or conceit, but in humility count others more significant than yourselves. Let each of you look not only to his own interests, but also to the interests of others. Have this mind among yourselves, which is yours in Christ Jesus." Philippians 2:1-5

"Strive for peace with everyone, and for the holiness without which no one will see the Lord." Hebrews 12:14

As you seek peace with others in your midst, may Paul's exhortation in Colossians 3:12–15 be at the center of your heart and mind:

Put on then, as God's chosen ones, holy and beloved, compassionate hearts, kindness, humility, meekness, and patience, bearing with one another and, if one has a complaint against another, forgiving each other; as the Lord has forgiven you, so you also must forgive. And above all these put on love, which binds everything together in perfect harmony. And let the peace of Christ rule in your hearts, to which indeed you were called in one body. And be thankful.

Extended Reading: Colossians 3

Peace in All Circumstances

DAY 26

DEVOTIONAL

Verses telling of the peace available to us in all circumstances are some of the most encouraging and powerful truths of Scripture. God longs for us to be children marked by the peace of our Father. He longs for us to have peace in the good and bad times because he remains faithful and good, always. He longs for us to be so founded in him that this world can't shake us.

*"Now may the Lord of peace himself give you peace
at all times in every way. The Lord be with you all."*

2 THESSALONIANS 3:16

You and I have every reason to live with the stresses and cares of the world save one: God dwells within us. 2 Thessalonians 3:16 says, *"Now may the Lord of peace himself give you peace at all times in every way. The Lord be with you all."* We serve the Lord of peace. The Holy Spirit who dwells within us is wholly peaceful. And Galatians 5:22 tells us that he will bear the fruit of peace in our lives if we simply live in continual communion with him.

Circumstances begin to rob us of our peace the minute we choose to live as if God isn't within us. Trials and tribulations will become all-consuming if we allow them to. You see, we are not to live with our physical eyes as our sole source of truth. God has granted us spiritual eyes and the ability to have faith in his faithfulness and goodness regardless of our circumstances. He's given us the ability to choose to live with union with him as our foundation. We are not alone. We are never alone. The God who authored Scripture, knows all of eternity, raised Christ from the dead, and empowered the disciples dwells within us, always.

You will only live with peace in this life to the level that you live out of the union you have with God. In every situation, God is with you, ready and willing to lead you, empower you, sustain you, and fill you with peace in response to your trust. John 14:27 says,

"Peace I leave with you; my peace I give to you. Not as the world gives do I give to you. Let not your hearts be troubled, neither let them be afraid." Peace is our portion. And this peace is not given as the world gives, based on the fickle nature of man and the ever-changing opinion of the world. Heavenly peace finds its source solely in the unchanging nature of our good and loving heavenly Father.

You and I are commanded by Jesus, *"Let not your hearts be troubled, neither let them be afraid"* (John 14:27). We must take captive our emotions and ground them in the unshakable nature of God. We must allow a direct connection from our hearts to the Holy Spirit who dwells within us, letting him speak to us, fill us, and direct our every moment.

The peace of God transcends anything we will experience on this earth. If we place our lives in the capable hands of our heavenly Father, we can trust that his perfect, pleasing plans will be done in our lives. Take time today to ground your peace in the unshakable nature of your heavenly Father. Take time to turn your eyes away from the world as your source of peace and set them instead on union with God. May the Holy Spirit reveal his nearness to you in mighty and powerful ways today as you open your heart and receive his loving presence.

131

GUIDED PRAYER

1. Meditate on the peace available to you in all circumstances.

"Peace I leave with you; my peace I give to you. Not as the world gives do I give to you. Let not your hearts be troubled, neither let them be afraid." John 14:27

"Now may the Lord of peace himself give you peace at all times in every way. The Lord be with you all." 2 Thessalonians 3:16

2. In what ways do you look to the world for your peace? Who or what holds the reigns on your emotions and peace?

3. Ask the Holy Spirit to reveal his nearness to you. Ask him to help you discover the union you already have with him. Take your eyes off the things of the world and establish your peace in God alone.

"Do you not know that you are God's temple and that God's Spirit dwells in you?" 1 Corinthians 3:16

"The Spirit of God has made me, and the breath of the Almighty gives me life." Job 33:4

"May the God of hope fill you with all joy and peace in believing, so that by the power of the Holy Spirit you may abound in hope." Romans 15:13

Learning to receive our peace from God alone is a process. When we've lived with the world as our emotional source it takes time to ground ourselves in God. But this is a process worth doing. God has unshakable peace in store for you every day regardless of the circumstances you face. He has love, joy, and steadfastness available to you in every trial and tribulation. Look to God as your source today and discover the abundant life available to you in him alone.

Extended Reading: John 14

Peace in Our Spirits

DAY 27

DEVOTIONAL

Ephesians 4:30 says, *"And do not grieve the Holy Spirit of God, by whom you were sealed for the day of redemption."* In the Holy Spirit, we have relationship with a God who feels, has joy and grief, is happy and unhappy, and has real thoughts and desires for the way we live our lives. The Spirit longs for us to live in communion with him, forsaking that which grieves his heart that we might experience the abundant life that only comes through wholehearted surrender to him. And it's because he has specific desires for the ways we should live that we have the potential to grieve his heart.

*"And do not grieve the Holy Spirit of God, by
whom you were sealed for the day of redemption."*

EPHESIANS 4:30

If we are to ever experience all that's available to us in this life, we must learn to pay attention to the feelings, thoughts, and desires of the God within us. We must seek and find peace in our spirits that comes from the peace of the Holy Spirit. Scripture makes a powerful and direct connection between obeying God's word and peace. Psalm 119:165 says, *"Great peace have those who love your law; nothing can make them stumble."* Isaiah 32:17 says, *"And the effect of righteousness will be peace, and the result of righteousness, quietness and trust forever."* And Psalm 34:14 says, *"Turn away from evil and do good; seek peace and pursue it."*

The desires of the Holy Spirit for our lives are perfectly aligned with Scripture. In fact, the Spirit longs to bring revelation to our hearts about how to apply and obey Scripture in our everyday lives. He longs to apply his words to our circumstances, situations, and thoughts that we might enjoy all the abundance that comes from obedience to God's word.

It's vital that we as believers living in union with God learn to take notice of how he feels, what he thinks, and where he's leading us. We must grow in our knowledge of how he speaks to us and leads us. If you feel unrest in your spirit that doesn't seem to make

sense, take time to ask God if he's speaking. If you feel weird about doing something, saying something, or thinking something, take a minute to ask God if he's trying to tell you something.

The use of Scripture is incredibly important in growing in peace with the Holy Spirit. It's so much easier to discern his thoughts and feelings if we have Scripture in our minds and hearts for him to point to. The greatest way to confirm that you are discerning the will of God is to ask him to bring back to mind a Scripture that goes along with his leading. God will never tell you to do something contrary to Scripture. He will never lead you in a direction that is not in perfect alignment with the words he's so perfectly given you in the Bible.

Learning to discern how the Holy Spirit thinks, feels, and leads is an absolutely crucial part of experiencing peace. Engage in the process of growing in relationship with the Spirit. Take notice of ways in which he might be speaking. Ask him to grow you in your ability to think, feel, and act in union with his will. You have a fully loving, powerful, faithful, and able God dwelling within you. May you experience the fullness of life that comes from peace between you and the Holy Spirit.

GUIDED PRAYER

1. Meditate on Scripture about the Holy Spirit. Ask the Holy Spirit to give you revelation about who he is through the words he's written.

"And do not grieve the Holy Spirit of God, by whom you were sealed for the day of redemption." Ephesians 4:30

"Or do you not know that your body is a temple of the Holy Spirit within you, whom you have from God? You are not your own." 1 Corinthians 6:19

"If you love me, you will keep my commandments. And I will ask the Father, and he will give you another Helper, to be with you forever, even the Spirit of truth, whom the world cannot receive, because it neither sees him nor knows him. You know him, for he dwells with you and will be in you." John 14:15-17

2. Ask the Holy Spirit to reveal his nearness to you. Ask him to teach you to discern how he feels, what he's thinking, and where he's leading.

3. Take time to rest in God's presence. Ask him whatever questions you have in your heart and let him teach you.

The Holy Spirit will never force his will, thoughts, or desires on us. He quietly beckons us into deeper relationship with him. But once we ask him for his will, he freely gives it. Learn to quiet your heart before him. Take time throughout your day to ask him how he feels about what you're doing. Make space for him to guide and direct you to the heart of the Father and his will for your life. May you be blessed with a substantial peace and joy today as you learn to live in obedience to the Spirit.

Extended Reading: Ephesians 4

Being a Person of Peace

DAY 28

DEVOTIONAL

One of the highest callings of God on the lives of his children is to be peacemakers. This world has no reason to have peace or give peace. While people are at war within themselves, striving to satisfy longings that can

*"Blessed are the peacemakers, for
they shall be called sons of God."*

MATTHEW 5:9

only be satisfied in God, we cannot expect them to bring peace around them. It's for this reason that you and I are called to make peace at all costs.

Matthew 5:9 says, *"Blessed are the peacemakers, for they shall be called sons of God."* To be a child of God is to make peace with everyone around you, regardless of how they treat you. Jesus sought peace at every turn. Even his turning of the tables was a cry for peace between man and his Father in heaven. The passionate condemnation of sin in Scripture exists to rid that which separates us from the peace of God. The fight for heavenly peace in the lives of men is a cause worth sacrifice, unfair treatment, and even persecution. For example, Scripture teaches us in 1 Peter 3:9-11,

Do not repay evil for evil or reviling for reviling, but on the contrary, bless, for to this you were called, that you may obtain a blessing. For "Whoever desires to love life and see good days, let him keep his tongue from evil and his lips from speaking deceit; let him turn away from evil and do good; let him seek peace and pursue it."

This world has no defense for unmerited blessing. It has no defense for the people of God loving unconditionally. When we choose not to repay evil for evil or revile when we've been reviled, we bring heaven to earth around us. No man or woman can live a truly peaceful life apart from the help of the Prince of Peace (Isaiah 9:6).

Jesus said in Matthew 5:38-42,

You have heard that it was said, "An eye for an eye and a tooth for a tooth." But I say to you, Do not resist the one who is evil. But if anyone slaps you on the right cheek, turn to him the other also. And if anyone would sue you and take your tunic, let him have your cloak as well. And if anyone forces you to go one mile, go with him two miles. Give to the one who begs from you, and do not refuse the one who would borrow from you.

The next time someone does evil to you, remember that it was us who did evil to Jesus. The next time someone *"slaps you on the right cheek,"* remember that it was us who shouted, *"Crucify him!"* when Jesus had done nothing wrong. It was our sin that put Jesus on the cross, and yet he willingly sacrificed his life that we might know peace. It's time for the people of God to choose to love others as Christ has loved us. It's time for us to lay down our rights in this life that others might come to know the love we've been shown. May you be filled with the courage to love unconditionally today as you encounter God's heart to fashion you into a peacemaker.

GUIDED PRAYER

1. Meditate on the call to be a peacemaker.

"Blessed are the peacemakers, for they shall be called sons of God." Matthew 5:9

"Turn away from evil and do good; seek peace and pursue it." Psalm 34:14

"For the kingdom of God is not a matter of eating and drinking but of righteousness and peace and joy in the Holy Spirit." Romans 14:17

2. What consistently keeps you from being a person of peace? What sense of justice or fairness keeps you from turning the other cheek?

3. Meditate on the actions of Jesus when he was unfairly treated. Why didn't he fight back? Ask the Holy Spirit to heal any wounds you have that keep you from loving unconditionally. Ask him to make you like Jesus that you would love people better today and make peace around you.

"You have heard that it was said, 'An eye for an eye and a tooth for a tooth.' But I say to you, Do not resist the one who is evil. But if anyone slaps you on the right cheek, turn to him the other also. And if anyone would sue you and take your tunic, let him have your cloak as well. And if anyone forces you to go one mile, go with him two miles. Give to the one who begs from you, and do not refuse the one who would borrow from you." Matthew 5:38-42

"Do not repay evil for evil or reviling for reviling, but on the contrary, bless, for to this you were called, that you may obtain a blessing. For 'Whoever desires to love life and see good days, let him keep his tongue from evil and his lips from speaking deceit; let him turn away from evil and do good; let him seek peace and pursue it.'" 1 Peter 3:9-11

Scripture never said that making peace would be easy. It also never said that it would come naturally. Being a peacemaker only comes from living out of a revelation of who Jesus is and who we are in him. It only comes from valuing God's heart over our own worldliness. There are not some of us who are peacemakers and others who are fighters. There are not some of us who are just meek and mild and others who aren't. We are all called to make peace. We are all called to turn the other cheek. We are all called to search out the will of God for our lives and choose his ways over our own or the world's. To choose to make peace is to live a lifestyle filled with the Spirit and all his fruit. May you abide in your heavenly Father today and experience the abundant life that comes from making peace all around you.

Extended Reading: 1 Peter 3

Living
for heaven

"For here we have no lasting city,
but we seek the city that is to come."
—Hebrews 13:14

As children of God, we have been given a new home and a new hope. May your heart be set aflame by the joy and purpose of living out God's command to live for heaven this week: "If then you have been raised with Christ, seek the things that are above, where Christ is, seated at the right hand of God. Set your minds on things that are above, not on things that are on earth. For you have died, and your life is hidden with Christ in God. When Christ who is your life appears, then you also will appear with him in glory." –Colossians 3:1-4

Jesus is the
Best Thing

DEVOTIONAL

Of all the wonders our Creator provides us, boundless and unadulterated relationship with Jesus vastly exceeds them all. Jesus is the best thing we will ever know. His love restores, satisfies, transforms, and heals. His grace empowers and brings transcendent peace. His nearness resolves the great fears of our hearts. And his Kingship calls us to a right lifestyle of living for heaven rather than a pursuit of that which is worldly and fleeting. Colossians 3:1-4 says,

"Therefore, since we are surrounded by so great a cloud of witnesses, let us also lay aside every weight, and sin which clings so closely, and let us run with endurance the race that is set before us, looking to Jesus, the founder and perfecter of our faith, who for the joy that was set before him endured the cross, despising the shame, and is seated at the right hand of the throne of God."

HEBREWS 12:1-2

If then you have been raised with Christ, seek the things that are above, where Christ is, seated at the right hand of God. Set your minds on things that are above, not on things that are on earth. For you have died, and your life is hidden with Christ in God. When Christ who is your life appears, then you also will appear with him in glory.

You and I have limited space in our hearts. When we choose to fill our lives with the things of the world, we crowd out that which will fill us with pure and abounding relationship with Jesus. It's for this reason Jesus said in Matthew 6:24, *"No one can serve two masters, for either he will hate the one and love the other, or he will be devoted to the one and despise the other. You cannot serve God and money."*

As disciples of Jesus, we must learn to lead different lives than others around us. Instead of looking to others as our standard for what is good or right,

we must look to Jesus. Instead of setting the bar for our lives by looking at successful people, even successful Christians, we must set our bar at living like Jesus. Jesus valued relationship with the Father above all else. He valued obedience to the Father's will above all other pursuits. Every breath he breathed was done to the glory of God the Father and in fulfillment of his plans, and you and I are to do the same.

To live for heaven is to throw off every weight that would hinder us from pursuing the fullness of relationship with Jesus. To live for heaven is to declare with our thoughts, actions, and emotions that Jesus truly is Lord of lords and King of kings and that he is worthy of our lives. To live for heaven is to make as much room in our hearts for Jesus as possible. Live for heaven today and discover the wealth of relationship and satisfaction available to you only through the sole pursuit of Jesus.

GUIDED PRAYER

1. Meditate on the principle of serving two masters. Allow Scripture to stir up your heart to pursue relationship with Jesus above all else. Renew your mind to what truly has value in this life.

"But seek first the kingdom of God and his righteousness, and all these things will be added to you. Therefore do not be anxious about tomorrow, for tomorrow will be anxious for itself. Sufficient for the day is its own trouble." Matthew 6:33-34

"Therefore, since we are surrounded by so great a cloud of witnesses, let us also lay aside every weight, and sin which clings so closely, and let us run with endurance the race that is set before us, looking to Jesus, the founder and perfecter of our faith, who for the joy that was set before him endured the cross, despising the shame, and is seated at the right hand of the throne of God." Hebrews 12:1-2

"The Lord is my shepherd; I shall not want." Psalm 23:1

2. What things of the world have you been pursuing? In what ways has the world crowded out space that was meant solely for the things of God?

"Do not be conformed to this world, but be transformed by the renewal of your mind, that by testing you may discern what is the will of God, what is good and acceptable and perfect." Romans 12:2

3. Ask the Lord to lead you to a lifestyle of living for heaven. Ask him to give you a vision of what it looks like to pursue relationship with him above all else. Commit to following his leadership to paths of righteousness and relationship and turn away from worldly cares and pursuits.

"Do not love the world or the things in the world. If anyone loves the world, the love of the Father is not in him. For all that is in the world—the desires of the flesh and the desires of the eyes and pride in possessions—is

not from the Father but is from the world. And the world is passing away along with its desires, but whoever does the will of God abides forever." 1 John 2:15-17

Living with a heavenly perspective takes time spent in God's presence, studying his word. It's unnatural to live in the world but not of the world (John 15:19). There are few to no people we encounter in our daily routine who truly live out this command. If we are going to fully pursue the abundant life to which we've been called, we must choose to live differently. If we are going to truly live for heaven, we must allow the Lord to daily renew our perspective on what matters. The life available to us through pursuing Jesus alone may be countercultural, but it is filled with adventure, wonder, satisfaction, and purpose. May you be filled with the courage to throw off the burdens of the world and live solely for Jesus today.

Extended Reading: 1 John 2

Life in Hope

DAY 30

The world is a fearful and unsatisfying place without the hope of eternal life with Jesus. Apart from the expectation that comes from the hope of heaven, our world is without cause for peace, celebration, or joy. There is life in hope. There is joy in hope. There is purpose in hope. Hope is to be at the foundation of all our decisions, emotions, and pursuits. Hope fills us with joy in the midst of trial and perseverance in the midst of failure. Hope guides us to abundant life.

"May the God of hope fill you with all joy and peace in believing, so that by the power of the Holy Spirit you may abound in hope."

ROMANS 15:13

Romans 8:24-25 says, *"For in this hope we were saved. Now hope that is seen is not hope. For who hopes for what he sees? But if we hope for what we do not see, we wait for it with patience."* We have the promise of eternal life in perfect, unveiled relationship with our Creator and Sustainer. The King of kings and Lord of lords waits patiently for the final redemption and restoration of all things (Revelation 21:1). He longs for the day when all pain, tears, disappointment, separation, and sin will end for good (Revelation 21:4). And he longs to fill us with the same hope and expectation he has within himself.

Romans 15:13 says, *"May the God of hope fill you with all joy and peace in believing, so that by the power of the Holy Spirit you may abound in hope."* Our heavenly Father longs to make us a people of hope. He longs for his followers to live a lifestyle that declares to the world, "This life is not all there is." He longs to fill us with a heavenly perspective that we might throw off pursuits of worldly pleasure and live for eternity with him.

Jesus said in Matthew 6:19-21, *"Do not lay up for yourselves treasures on earth, where moth and rust destroy and where thieves break in and steal, but lay up for yourselves treasures in heaven, where neither moth nor rust destroys and where thieves do not break in and steal. For where your treasure is, there your heart will be also."* The hope of eternal life with our Father is to be the guiding light set ever before us. Where have you set your hope? Where do the treasures of your heart lie? Placing our hope in heaven secures the treasures of our hearts with our heavenly Father for all of eternity. In contrast, when we treasure the things of the world, that which we accumulate will pass away as quickly as it came.

Take time in guided prayer to allow the Lord to fill you with a fresh hope for the age that is to come. Allow your perspectives to shift in light of the glory of an eternity spent in total communion with the Creator. May the hope of heaven guide you to a lifestyle of storing up your treasures, and therefore your heart, with your heavenly Father.

GUIDED PRAYER

1. Meditate on importance of hope. Allow Scripture to shift your perspectives and pursuits to living for heaven.

"For I know the plans I have for you, declares the Lord, plans for welfare and not for evil, to give you a future and a hope." Jeremiah 29:11

"The hope of the righteous brings joy, but the expectation of the wicked will perish." Proverbs 10:28

2. Where have you placed your hope in the things of the world? What have you been looking to in order to satisfy your longings that is fleeting and temporary?

"Do not lay up for yourselves treasures on earth, where moth and rust destroy and where thieves break in and steal, but lay up for yourselves treasures in heaven, where neither moth nor rust destroys and where thieves do not break in and steal. For where your treasure is, there your heart will be also." Matthew 6:19-21

3. Ask the Lord to help you place your hope in heaven alone. Choose to live your life for your heavenly Father instead of seeking worldly success and satisfaction. Ask the Holy Spirit to reveal to you ways in which you can rid yourself of the world and receive the hope of heaven.

"The thief comes only to steal and kill and destroy. I came that they may have life and have it abundantly." John 10:10

May Romans 5:2-5 be your anthem of hope today:

Through him we have also obtained access by faith into this grace in which we stand, and we rejoice in hope of the glory of God. More than that, we rejoice in our sufferings, knowing that suffering produces endurance, and endurance produces character, and character produces hope, and hope does not put us to shame, because God's love has been poured into our hearts through the Holy Spirit who has been given to us.

Extended Reading: Romans 15

Marked by Joy

DAY 31

DEVOTIONAL

C.S. Lewis said, "All joy emphasizes our pilgrim status; always reminds, beckons, awakens desire. Our best havings are wantings." As pilgrims on the journey to boundless communion with our heavenly Father, we are called to be marked by a sustaining and transcendent joy. Our God is a God of joy. He is the creator of fun and the giver of abundant life. He longs for his children to taste and see his goodness (Psalm 34:8). He longs for us to open our hearts, cast off the cares of this world, and receive the joy that comes from living for heaven.

"The hope of the righteous brings joy, but the expectation of the wicked will perish."

PROVERBS 10:28

Romans 14:17 says, *"For the kingdom of God is not a matter of eating and drinking but of righteousness and peace and joy in the Holy Spirit."* Psalm 16:11 says, *"You make known to me the path of life; in your presence there is fullness of joy; at your right hand are pleasures forevermore."* Proverbs 10:28 says, *"The hope of the righteous brings joy, but the expectation of the wicked will perish."* We serve a joyful King. There is no greater joy than living in the fullness of relationship available to us in Christ. To live for heaven is to throw off whatever weight would entangle us to the depravity of this world and seek sustaining joy that comes down from heaven to fill our hearts.

Our Father cares deeply about the concerns of this world. He weeps over the lost. He becomes angry over the works of the enemy. He is deeply saddened when we choose the fleeting and unsatisfying ways of the world over his fulfilling and perfect plans. But in the midst of all his emotions, he is joyfully expectant for the age that is to come. He sees the depravity and wounds and celebrates that one day soon it will all be redeemed. He is elated over the day that *"he will wipe away every tear from their eyes, and death shall be no more, neither shall there be mourning, nor crying, nor pain anymore, for the former things have passed away"* (Revelation 21:4). And there is sustaining joy available to us this side of heaven if we will allow him to fill us with his perspective.

James 1:2-4 says, *"Count it all joy, my brothers, when you meet trials of various kinds, for you know that the testing of your faith produces steadfastness. And let steadfastness have its full effect, that you may be perfect and complete, lacking in nothing."* If we will allow the Lord to redeem the trials and testing we endure in this life, we will begin to bear the fruit of joy in the midst of any circumstance. Unshakable joy is our portion. The heart of our Father is to make us a people marked by the joy of heaven. Take time today in guided prayer to throw off whatever is keeping you from experiencing the joy of the Lord. Rest in his presence and search out his heart. May you be a child marked by the joy of your heavenly Father today.

GUIDED PRAYER

1. Meditate on the importance and availability of joy to you. Allow Scripture to fill your heart with a longing to pursue continual joy.

"For you shall go out in joy and be led forth in peace; the mountains and the hills before you shall break forth into singing, and all the trees of the field shall clap their hands." Isaiah 55:12

"For the kingdom of God is not a matter of eating and drinking but of righteousness and peace and joy in the Holy Spirit." Romans 14:17

2. What is keeping you from experiencing joy? What is weighing you down today? Ask for the Lord's help in throwing off that which is robbing you of his joy. Ask him to guide you to a path of unshakable joy today.

"Count it all joy, my brothers, when you meet trials of various kinds, for you know that the testing of your faith produces steadfastness. And let steadfastness have its full effect, that you may be perfect and complete, lacking in nothing." James 1:2-4

"For our heart is glad in him, because we trust in his holy name." Psalm 33:21

3. Take time to rest in the presence of your Father and search out his heart. Ask him to share with you his perspective for your life. Ask him to help you care about only the things he cares about.

"You make known to me the path of life; in your presence there is fullness of joy; at your right hand are pleasures forevermore." Psalm 16:11

"You have put more joy in my heart than they have when their grain and wine abound." Psalm 4:7

C.S Lewis is also quoted as saying, "Joy is the serious business of heaven." We are not to be flippant about our joy. To be marked by joy is to allow the Holy Spirit to bear fruit in our lives. When we have genuine joy in the midst of trials and troubles, we declare to the world the unchanging and tangible goodness of our heavenly Father. When we meet challenges head-on with joy, we declare with our attitudes the hope we have for the age that is to come. Pursue joy wholeheartedly today and declare with your life the principles of God's kingdom so that others might come to restored relationship with their Creator.

Extended Reading: Psalm 33

A Lifetime of Love

DAY 32

DEVOTIONAL

We belong to a kingdom built not by the blood, sweat, and tears of servants but by the wounds and scars of a loving and sacrificial King. As disciples of Jesus we have been granted access into a lifetime of giving and receiving unconditional love. Our Savior willingly laid down his life that we might know the love of our heavenly Father throughout this life and all eternity. John 15:9-13 says,

*"As the Father has loved me, so have
I loved you. Abide in my love."*

JOHN 15:9

As the Father has loved me, so have I loved you. Abide in my love. If you keep my commandments, you will abide in my love, just as I have kept my Father's commandments and abide in his love. These things I have spoken to you, that my joy may be in you, and that your joy may be full. This is my commandment, that you love one another as I have loved you. Greater love has no one than this, that someone lay down his life for his friends.

To live for heaven is to abide in a lifetime of constant and tangible love from the Father so that we might live healed and able to pour out genuine love to others. This life is all about love. Jesus boiled down all the commandments into loving God and loving people. If we truly desire to live in obedience to God's commands, we must live with a heavenly perspective. 1 John 4:7 says, *"Beloved, let us love one another, for love is from God, and whoever loves has been born of God and knows God."* To live for the world is to maintain an attitude of selfishness and pursue fleeting and insincere affections. To live for heaven is to daily say yes to being born of God and to pursue knowing the Father. To know our Creator is to know love itself. And when we experience the love of our Father, we will be transformed into instruments of his love for all those around us.

God longs to give us a heavenly perspective today that we might receive the fullness of his love and in return love him and others. 1 John 4:19 says, *"We love because he first loved us."* Living for heaven starts with letting God love us. It starts with carving out space in our daily routine to rest in the knowledge of our Father's love and allow it to transform, redeem, and heal us. We all carry wounds that need to be touched by the love of our Father.

It's only after being loved by God that we can truly love others. Without encounters with the heart of the Father, we are incapable of living selflessly. Pride is the natural state of all those who aren't consistently encountering the transformative power of the Holy Spirit. But through God's grace and receiving a heavenly perspective, we can step outside ourselves and the fleshly desires of this world and truly love others with the heart of God.

Take time in guided prayer to let your heavenly Father love you today. Let go of any roots of pride that are keeping you from loving him and others. And ask the Holy Spirit to guide you into a lifestyle of loving others with the love you've been shown in Christ Jesus.

161

GUIDED PRAYER

1. Take time to receive the love of your heavenly Father. Meditate on Scripture that will fill you with the knowledge of his love. Ask him to reveal his nearness and wait on his calming and peaceful presence.

"We love because he first loved us." 1 John 4:19

"As the Father has loved me, so have I loved you. Abide in my love." John 15:9

2. Ask the Holy Spirit to reveal to you anything that is keeping you from living a lifestyle of being loved and loving others.

3. How would the Holy Spirit guide you into a lifestyle of loving others today? In what ways have you been loved so that you can turn around and love others? Who needs grace and forgiveness today? Who needs a loving friend or a kind stranger? Who needs to hear the message of reconciliation and hope that you've found in Jesus?

"If anyone says, 'I love God,' and hates his brother, he is a liar; for he who does not love his brother whom he has seen cannot love God whom he has not seen. And this commandment we have from him: whoever loves God must also love his brother." 1 John 4:20–21

"Let all that you do be done in love." 1 Corinthians 16:14

"Beloved, let us love one another, for love is from God, and whoever loves has been born of God and knows God." 1 John 4:7

For the majority of my relationship with God up to this point, I didn't know what it meant to truly experience God's love. I didn't know that God could tangibly affect my emotions, mood, purpose, and perspective with his presence. It was only once I began to consistently make time and space to let God love me that my life began to be transformed and healed and I began to walk in freedom. It was only once I began to consistently encounter God's heart that I was filled with a longing to love others. There is nothing more important or foundational to this life than experiencing the love of your heavenly Father. May you discover the wealth of affections your Father has for you as you carve out space to encounter him throughout your day today.

Extended Reading: John 15

Heaven on Earth

DEVOTIONAL

In Matthew 6:9-13 Jesus taught us to pray: *"Our Father in heaven, hallowed be your name. Your kingdom come, your will be done, on earth as it is in heaven. Give us this day our daily bread, and forgive us our debts, as we also have forgiven our debtors. And lead us not into temptation, but deliver us from evil."*

*"Our Father in heaven, hallowed be
your name. Your kingdom come, your will be
done, on earth as it is in heaven."*

MATTHEW 6:9-10

To seek God's kingdom coming to earth is to declare our great need for God's presence, provision, love, and redemption. We have been given a mandate of the highest importance from our King of kings. We are to carry the kingdom of God with us everywhere we go and release this kingdom through everything we do. We are called by Jesus to bring heaven to earth.

In Matthew 16:19 Jesus tells his disciples, *"I will give you the keys of the kingdom of heaven, and whatever you bind on earth shall be bound in heaven, and whatever you loose on earth shall be loosed in heaven."* What would it look like for the people of God to release the kingdom of heaven everywhere they go? What would it look like for even just a few of us to truly say yes to the calling of God on our lives to live for more than just worldly pleasure and comfort, to step outside of ourselves and live with an eternal perspective?

You are made to make an eternal impact far greater than you can imagine. God has placed within you keys to the doors of heaven, and he longs to use you to release his love, grace, peace, mercy, and redemption to others in desperate need of him. He longs to call you out from the daily grind of life into a higher pursuit of seeing the earth transformed by his goodness.

Seeing heaven come to earth all starts with declaring your need of God. It all starts with drawing a circle around yourself and allowing God to transform you from the inside out. You are not called to minister to others in your own strength. You are not called to figure out how to best love people. You aren't even called to muster up a desire to bring God's kingdom to earth. All the weight of eternal impact rests on the shoulders of your heavenly Father. All that is required of you is to take time to let God love you, fill you with the desires of his heart, and follow his leadership into the fulfillment of those desires.

God wants to take your five loaves of bread and two fish and multiply it to feed the souls of thousands. Say yes to partnering with the Holy Spirit, and allow God to use you to change the world by bringing his kingdom to earth through simple acts of love and obedience. Take time in guided prayer to allow God's word and his Spirit to teach you, empower you, and release you into the calling of bringing heaven to earth today.

165

GUIDED PRAYER

1. Meditate on the calling to bring God's kingdom to earth.
Allow Scripture to lay a foundation for powerful works of God's Spirit to pour out through your life.

"I will give you the keys of the kingdom of heaven, and whatever you bind on earth shall be bound in heaven, and whatever you loose on earth shall be loosed in heaven." Matthew 16:19

"In the same way, let your light shine before others, so that they may see your good works and give glory to your Father who is in heaven." Matthew 5:16

2. What keys has God given you to release his kingdom?
What spiritual gifts has he given you? What ways do you best love people? How has he used you in the past to reveal his love?

3. Ask the Holy Spirit to teach you how to bring heaven to earth today. Ask him to fill you up that you might pour out. Ask him to tear down any walls that would keep you from loving him and others well.

Being used by God to bring heaven to earth is meant to be a part of the normal, daily Christian life. We are called to more than simply working a job, going to school, hanging out with friends, and trying to enjoy life. No matter what job you work, God wants to bring the kingdom to earth through you. No matter who your friends are or where you find yourself, God wants to bring the kingdom to earth everywhere around you. If you will say yes every day to the adventure of being used by God, your life will begin to take on a whole new purpose so much more fulfilling than anything you've previously experienced. May you live to see God's kingdom come to earth through your life today.

Extended Reading: Luke 9

167

Things Unseen

DAY 34

DEVOTIONAL

We have been trained through the prideful perspective of many that we are only to look to and believe that which we can see and physically experience here on earth. We're told that there couldn't possibly be more to life than what we've seen because the unseen can't

*"We look not to the things that are seen
but to the things that are unseen. For the things
that are seen are transient, but the things that
are unseen are eternal."*

2 CORINTHIANS 4:18

be experienced in the physical. What a self-centered perspective! Why do we have to know and be able to presently experience all there is in order for it to be real? Why are we, with our limited capacities, the ultimate judge in the debate of what is real and important? In Ephesians 1:18–20, Paul wrote to the church in Ephesus praying,

Having the eyes of your hearts enlightened, that you may know what is the hope to which he has called you, what are the riches of his glorious inheritance in the saints, and what is the immeasurable greatness of his power toward us who believe, according to the working of his great might that he worked in Christ when he raised him from the dead and seated him at his right hand in the heavenly places.

"Having the eyes of your hearts enlightened . . . ." What does it mean for our hearts to have eyes? And what does it mean for those eyes to be enlightened? The truth is that all of us are given spiritual eyes. All of us know and experience things that can't be physically seen. We've all received and given some type of love. We've all had an intuition or belief that couldn't be

physically proven. And as believers, we've been filled with the Holy Spirit who longs to guide us to a perspective that far exceeds the span of this world.

2 Corinthians 4:18 says, *"We look not to the things that are seen but to the things that are unseen. For the things that are seen are transient, but the things that are unseen are eternal."* Our Savior is calling us to a life lived for that which is unseen: the eternal. He is calling us out of the cycle of worldly pursuit into a greater calling of eternal significance. To live for heaven is to cast off that which is fleeting and temporary and seek that which can only be found with our heavenly Father.

Take time in guided prayer to look to that which is unseen. Ask the Holy Spirit to enlighten the eyes of your heart. Ask him to give you spiritual insight into your own life and the lives of others that you might call all those around you to live for heaven. Cast off those pursuits which tie you down to this world, and ask the Spirit to guide you into a lifestyle of seeking the kingdom of God above all else. May you discover the abundant life available to you in the Spirit as you worship your Father in both spirit and truth today.

GUIDED PRAYER

1. Meditate on the importance of looking to that which is unseen. Allow Scripture to fill your heart with a longing to live for heaven.

"We look not to the things that are seen but to the things that are unseen. For the things that are seen are transient, but the things that are unseen are eternal." 2 Corinthians 4:18

"Now faith is the assurance of things hoped for, the conviction of things not seen. For by it the people of old received their commendation. By faith we understand that the universe was created by the word of God, so that what is seen was not made out of things that are visible." Hebrews 11:1-3

"By faith Noah, being warned by God concerning events as yet unseen, in reverent fear constructed an ark for the saving of his household. By this he condemned the world and became an heir of the righteousness that comes by faith." Hebrews 11:7

2. Ask the Holy Spirit to reveal to you any pursuits which are solely fleeting and temporary. Write down any ways in which you have not been looking to the unseen enough.

3. Ask the Spirit to enlighten the eyes of your heart that you might experience all that God has for you today.

"Having the eyes of your hearts enlightened, that you may know what is the hope to which he has called you, what are the riches of his glorious inheritance in the saints, and what is the immeasurable greatness of his power toward us who believe, according to the working of his great might that he worked in Christ when he raised him from the dead and seated him at his right hand in the heavenly places." Ephesians 1:18-20

Looking to that which is unseen is the door through which we experience the fullness of God's presence available to us on the earth. As Jesus taught us, *"God is spirit,"* and to truly experience him we must cultivate a lifestyle of opening the eyes of our hearts. Our Father longs to lead us to a lifestyle of continual and transformational encounters with him. He longs to meet us at the doors of our hearts every morning that we might let him in to love us, speak to us, fill us, and transform us. May looking to that which is unseen guide you into deeper and more impactful encounters with the living God.

Extended Reading: 2 Corinthians 4

The Day Is Approaching

DEVOTIONAL

Have you ever counted down the days until you'll be able to see a good friend? Have you ever felt anticipation and butterflies as the time separating you and a loved one grows smaller? I grew up knowing that I should feel this way about heaven, but if I am honest I never truly felt the same anticipation and longings for perfect communion with my Savior as I did for a dear friend.

*"But concerning that day and hour no one knows, not even
the angels of heaven, nor the Son, but the Father only."*

MATTHEW 24:36

I think the idea of an eternal worship service scared me. Having to worship God for all eternity sounded far worse than spending time hanging out with my best friends here on earth. The truth is I didn't have a true, tangible revelation of God's love for me. I didn't have an understanding of the incredible, deep, overwhelming satisfaction I feel when my heart touches God's heart in worship. I honestly didn't know the person of Jesus enough to want to spend all of eternity with him. Jesus teaches in Matthew 25:1-13,

Then the kingdom of heaven will be like ten virgins who took their lamps and went to meet the bridegroom. Five of them were foolish, and five were wise. For when the foolish took their lamps, they took no oil with them, but the wise took flasks of oil with their lamps. As the bridegroom was delayed, they all became drowsy and slept. But at midnight there was a cry, "Here is the bridegroom! Come out to meet him." Then all those virgins rose and trimmed their lamps. And the foolish said to the wise, "Give us some of your oil, for our lamps are going out." But the wise answered, saying, "Since there will not be enough for us and for you, go rather to the dealers and buy for yourselves." And while they were going to buy, the bridegroom came, and those who were ready went in with him to the marriage feast, and the door was shut. Afterward the other virgins came also, saying, "Lord, lord, open to us." But he answered, "Truly, I say to you, I do not know you." Watch therefore, for you know neither the day nor the hour.

The day of Jesus' return is approaching. Matthew 24:36 says, *"But concerning that day and hour no one knows, not even the angels of heaven, nor the Son, but the Father only."* Our Savior, the King of kings, will return with love in his heart for all those who have come to know him. The question before us today is this: are we like the five wise virgins who have prepared ourselves? Are our lamps burning with the intimacy of unveiled relationship with our Creator while here on the earth? Are we preparing for the return of our King by cultivating a lifestyle of love for both our bridegroom and others around us?

I've spent most of my life declaring I knew God by going to church, going on mission trips, saying the right things, and trying to do nothing wrong. My actions represented fear and a desire for inclusion in the Christian culture more than actual love and desire for Christ himself. Take time in guided prayer to truly analyze your heart. There is abundant grace today for wherever you find yourself in relation to your Savior. Be honest with yourself and look at how you feel about heaven. Are you prepared for the return of the King or living for the earth over heaven? Is the oil of relationship with Jesus in your lamp or are your fumes running out with the cares and pursuits of the world? May the Holy Spirit draw each of us into greater depths of intimacy with Jesus until the day our bridegroom returns.

GUIDED PRAYER

1. Meditate on the parable of the ten virgins. Allow Scripture to stir your heart toward deeper relationship with Jesus.

"Then the kingdom of heaven will be like ten virgins who took their lamps and went to meet the bridegroom. Five of them were foolish, and five were wise. For when the foolish took their lamps, they took no oil with them, but the wise took flasks of oil with their lamps. As the bridegroom was delayed, they all became drowsy and slept. But at midnight there was a cry, 'Here is the bridegroom! Come out to meet him.' Then all those virgins rose and trimmed their lamps. And the foolish said to the wise, 'Give us some of your oil, for our lamps are going out.' But the wise answered, saying, 'Since there will not be enough for us and for you, go rather to the dealers and buy for yourselves.' And while they were going to buy, the bridegroom came, and those who were ready went in with him to the marriage feast, and the door was shut. Afterward the other virgins came also, saying, 'Lord, lord, open to us.' But he answered, 'Truly, I say to you, I do not know you.' Watch therefore, for you know neither the day nor the hour." Matthew 25:1–13

2. Are you prepared for the return of Jesus? Truly look at your heart. What longings are driving you? Are you living for heaven or pursuing the things of the world? Is the oil of intimacy with Jesus in your lamp or are you running on the fumes of cultural Christianity?

3. Ask the Holy Spirit to guide you into greater depths of relationship with Jesus. Ask him to reveal to you the depths of God's love and grace.

God has a plan to guide you to a path of greater relationship with him if you will simply choose to follow his leadership. If you will daily say yes to him over the world, you will begin to feel a fire growing in your heart for Jesus' return. Once we experience the relationship with God we were created for, nothing else truly satisfies. His love is greater, purer, more real, and more powerful than anything else we will ever experience. Choose today to follow the leadership of the Spirit and grow in intimacy with the King who laid down his life for you to know his love.

Extended Reading: Matthew 25